Psychological Principles and the Black Experience

Lawrence N. Houston

UNIVERSITY
PRESS OF
AMERICA

Lanham • New York • London

University Press of America®, Inc.
4720 Boston Way
Lanham, Maryland 20706

3 Henrietta Street
London WC2E 8LU England

Printed in the United States of America
British Cataloging in Publication Information Available

Library of Congress Cataloging-in-Publication Data

Houston, Lawrence N., 1928-
Psychological principles and the Black experience
/ Lawrence N. Houston.
p. cm.
Includes bibliographical references and index.
1. Afro-Americans—Psychology. I. Title.
E185.625.H68 1990 155.8'496073—dc20 90–41492 CIP

ISBN 0–8191–7956–6 (cloth : alk. paper)
ISBN 0–8191–7957–4 (pbk. : alk. paper)

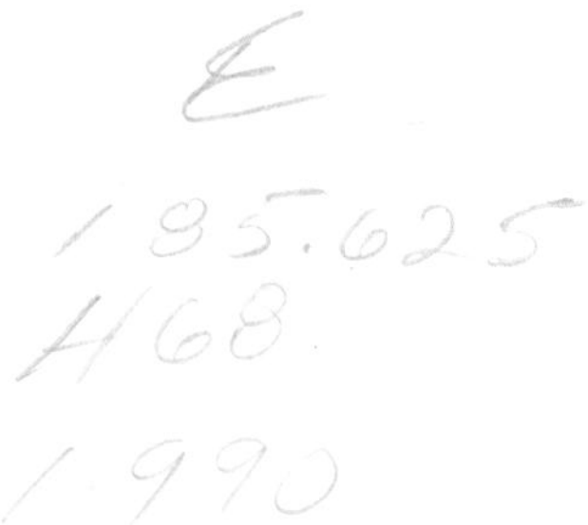

The paper used in this publication meets the minimum requirements of American National Standard for Information Sciences—Permanence of Paper for Printed Library Materials, ANSI Z39.48–1984.

Dedicated to my sons,
Geoffrey and Charleton

ACKNOWLEDGEMENTS

The author would like to express his gratitude to Dr. Deborah White of the Rutgers University History Department for her extremely helpful suggestions regarding the manuscript's treatment of Black history. Also, he would like to thank Ms. Adaya Henis, not only for her proofreading, editing and indexing, but also for her valuable suggestions. In addition, the author would like to express his appreciation for the dedicated secretarial assistance provided by Ms. Io-Aurelia Duncan, Mrs. Dolores Hovick and Ms. Peggy Gilchrist.

Table of Contents

Preface

As an outgrowth of the civil rights movement of the 1960s, Black scholars, scientists, academicians, and professional practitioners have developed a body of knowledge revealing clear distinctions between Black behavior and White behavior. This information has shown that these behavioral differences, rather than representing deficits, are the predictable results of the same principles and concepts that apply to all human beings. In this connection, we should be aware that in spite of the distinctness and singularity of the Black experience in the United States, the basic tenets and rudiments of psychological functioning are universal (Grier & Cobbs, cited in Guthrie, 1970). Therefore, the apparent discrepancy between the psychology of Blacks and Whites lies not with fundamental axioms but with their relative applicability. Given the African genesis, followed by the experience of slavery and subsequent oppression, the environmental impingements on Black Americans are recognized as having resulted in a neo-culture quite different from that of the Eurocentric norm.

A child's learning to read, for example, might be explained in terms of operant conditioning, social learning theory, classical conditioning, or some combination of the three. However, the qualitative and quantitative nature of the learning experience would vary according to a wide range of culturally related factors. These factors necessarily cause differential responses for Blacks and Whites. Similarly, abnormal behavior such as suicide could be traceable to "anomie" (Durkheim, 1951), a fatalistic predisposition (Breed, 1970) or interpersonal deprivation (Reynolds et al., 1975), regardless of the victim's race. But the actual components and parameters of the causal factors would be culturally relative and essentially invisible to one who does not share the relevant frame of reference.

Although most of the literature on Black psychology during the past decade has both contributed to and reflected a greater understanding of these differences, most major works relate only a small number of psychological principles and concepts to the Black experience. Self-esteem, achievement, personality, psychopathology, language development, and psychotherapy all have been related, separately and in various combinations, to the Black experience. Yet, such fundamental rudiments as perception, frustration and adjustment, normality, and the principles of learning (including modeling, classical conditioning and operant conditioning) never have been focused, as specifically identified concepts, on the behavior and mental processes of Black Americans, in a single volume.

The purpose of the present volume, therefore, is twofold: (1) to apply directly to the Black experience previously omitted psychological concepts and principles, and (2) to integrate these with previously presented material into one comprehensive volume that will serve as a general introduction to Black psychology.

CHAPTER ONE

A Brief Look at the Past

It is significantly through systematic investigation of factors impinging on our life conditions that we as a people will purposefully advance. (Boykin, Franklin, & Yates, 1979, p. 18)

Because the history of Black psychology is linked inextricably to the psychohistory of both Africa and Black America, and in view of the importance of past events in the lives of Africans, there is reinforcement of the observation by Jones that "in order to understand a people, one must first grasp and look into their past. The past will usually enable one to make a fair prediction of their present" (1978, p. 24). A review of the African heritage, then, would seem to provide the essential context within which psychology in relation to Blacks should be viewed. Although an exhaustive retracing is beyond the scope of this volume, it should be noted that present-day Black scholars are unearthing the richness of the Black American's African heritage in greater depth and wider scope than did previous researchers. In so doing, these scholars are dispelling the myths of a hereditary cultural destitution.

African Culture

The less recent view of Africa described it as the "dark continent," with virtually no civilization and no history until the coming of the Europeans. This image of Africa was well-suited to the proponents of slavery, and Black Americans were expected to be grateful to the White man for having been liberated, through slavery, from savagery and illiteracy. In perpetuation of this erroneous conceptualization, textbooks assigned to Black American school children as late as the 1940s reflected the "fact" (taken from the seventh edition of the *Encyclopaedia Britannica*) that Africa was a continent "practically without history and possessing no records from which such a history might be constructed" (Foner, 1975, p. 16).

That the myths regarding African history have a persistent life is indicated by several statements taken from a textbook on the slave trade, published in 1972. After mentioning the wealth and splendor of the Mali, Songhai, and ancient Ghana empires, the authors state:

> There were, however, notable gaps in the African cultures, and it was the gaps that impressed the Europeans. The Negro peoples had never devised a written langauge that became widely known (although the Vai of Sierra Leone, a branch of the great Mandingo family, reduced their own speech to writing toward the end of the eighteenth century). They had never invented the wheel or the plow, and in most technological matters even the more advanced African peoples were little removed from the early iron age. (Mannix & Cowley, p. 12)

Earlier in the same chapter, these historians report that:

> Africans south of the Sahara are divided by ethnologists into five main groups, only two of which played an important part in the slave trade. The most convenient names for the groups are Bushmanoid Pygmoid, Mongoloid, Caucasoid, and Negroid. In the desert regions of southern Africa are the Bushmanoids, yellow-brown in color, with "peppercorn" hair (kinking so tightly that it leaves bare areas on the scalp). The true Bushmen are usually less than five feet tall, but the Hottentots, who are partly Bushmen by descent, stand nearly a head taller. Both peoples are frequently steatopygic, that is possessed of huge buttocks which store up nourishment much as does a camel's hump. (P. 7)

One of the few scholars in the first half of the twentieth century to present a positive picture of Africa was Herskovits (1935), whose accounting has been verified and supplemented by more recent investigators (e.g. Davidson, 1961; DaSilva, 1969; Fulks, 1969; Comer, 1972; Foner, 1975; Burkey, 1978). These researchers give us the picture of Africa that is presented below.

Africa is inhabited by many peoples living in many different areas and having a variety of physical features and characteristics. Moreover, ever since the 1920s, archeological, paleontological, and anthropological evidence has shown that Africa, rather than any other continent, was the original home of the human family. This family is more than nineteen million years old, and its oldest member is

Kenyapithicus, who lived in the highlands of western Kenya nearly twenty million years ago (Leakey, cited in Foner, 1975). The continent is four times the size of the continental United States and consists of several geographical regions. Although various scholars have postulated from two to fifty geographical and/or cultural regions on the African continent, special attention should be given to the West Coast, the source of most of the slaves brought to the New World. In that area, more than anywhere else in Africa, the population density was most intense, the economic life most complex, and the technological and artistic developments the most advanced. The bronzes of Benin, the brasswork of Dahomey, the weaving of the Ashanti, and the woodcarving of Dahomey, Nigeria, and the Ivory Coast were superlatively developed. Particularly ubiquitous were the basketry and ironwork. Also found were the highly developed religions, a highly developed ancestral cult, and the arrangement of interpersonal relationships into highly complex social and political organizations. Some of the highly organized kingdoms of this region antedated Medieval times—for example, the kingdoms of Benin, Dahomey, and Ashanti.

In spite of the differences found among the regional cultures of Black Africa, there were marked similarities, especially when the continent was considered as a whole and its cultures were contrasted with those of other continents. Most salient among these commonalities was the content of the folklore, which could be subdivided into the three categories of animal stories, historical tales, and sacred myths. Another common feature throughout the cultures of Black Africa was the highly developed political organization, which involved an orderly legalism. This highly structured arrangement invalidates the often-held view of African society as one where quarrels erupted regularly, resulting in spontaneous battles, or where the strong overpower the weak at will. Such impulsiveness did not apply to any of the African groups. Herskovits relates that:

> Here the administration of justice is marked by well-ordered court procedure, where cases are presented with arguments from plaintiff and defendant, where widely-understood and accepted penalties exist for given types of crime, and where a system of appeals from lower to higher courts prevails. Among some tribes, furthermore, provision is made for plaintiff and defendant to be represented by those skilled in presentation of cases in court. In the presentation of these cases, another folkloristic form, the proverb, figures largely, for the aphorisms are introduced to make a case, cited in much the same manner as lawyers in European tribunals cite volumes

:r procedure to establish the necessary precedents. . 229)

Still another commonality among all African cultures was the emphasis on religion. This focus pervaded all aspects of African life. In marriage, birth, planting crops, taking a journey, hunting, and so on, the good will of the gods and ancestors had to be obtained. The method of worship involved ceremonialism, which included singing and dancing to the rhythms of drums.

Slavery in Africa

Historians seem to agree that slavery was in existence in most areas of Africa before the Europeans arrived on the continent. However, slavery in Africa was different from that which existed in other civilizations and was vastly unlike the slavery that developed in the New World. Prior to the European incursions, slaves in Africa were obtained from three primary sources: (1) prisoners of war; (2) debtors who pawned themselves as security for loans; and (3) convicted lawbreakers who were sentenced to slavery as punishment for their crimes. However, slaves often were considered to be members of the master's family. Frequently slaves were adopted by their masters and were given free status. Within certain cultures, slaves could marry free people (even royalty), and some even acquired ownership of other slaves. Among the Ashanti, slaves had rights that were not very different from those of any Ashanti free man; and in Benin, slaves could earn enough to purchase their freedom. Among the Yoruba and Hausa, slaves often were chosen by the rulers to occupy high positions. Most notably, the Kings of Dahomey "sometimes selected the son of a favorite slave wife to succeed to the throne" (Foner, 1975, p. 93). Furthermore, the labor of the slave in Africa was no greater than that of other Africans, even their masters, who often worked side by side with their slaves. Also, the clothing and the lodging of the slave were the same as for anyone else, although slaves generally were not permitted to eat with the free Africans.

The trading of slaves also was practiced in Africa prior to the European encroachment. To fill the harems of wealthy Asians, to supply domestic servants, or to provide workers for the Arab plantations, there was some trading in slaves with Asia and North Africa. Although slaves did become an important "commodity" within the Arab empire in the first half of the nineteenth century, this exportation was not the major commercial enterprise, given the greater value of ivory and gold. Also, the dangers of crossing the Sahara desert (where many slaves died), the scarcity of mines to be exploited, and the relatively small number of plantations all militated against the exportation of slaves to foreign territories.

Recognizing that Africa knew something of slavery and slave trading before the invasions of the Europeans, Foner (1975) reminds us that:

> Although the buying and selling of slaves had existed in Africa before the Europeans arrived, the institution of slavery was not so firmly established that the coming of foreign traders with a demand for labor led naturally and automatically to an organized trade in slaves for export. The expansion of Europe and the coming of the Europeans to Africa in the late fifteenth century, and especially in the sixteenth century, profoundly transformed African slavery and the slave trade. (P. 94)

The Beginning of the European Slave Trade

The transportation of slaves from Africa to Europe and eventually to the New World developed from the desire of the Western Europeans to locate new trade routes to India, China, and the Eastern seas, in order to avoid passing through the Islam-controlled Turkish strongholds.

In addition, Portugal, which in 1249 had rid itself of its last Muslim enclave, sought to spread Christianity by locating a legendary Christian empire (the land of Prester John) that supposedly was powerful enough to help Europeans subdue all of the Muslim infidels (Foner, 1975). Because the voyage of Marco Polo had determined that Prester John was not in either China or India, the seekers turned to Africa. Subsequently, Portuguese forces invaded Africa and captured the Moroccan seaport of Ceuta. By the mid 1400s, Portugal had ventured along the African Coast to Senegal. Though usually returning to Portugal with ivory, gold, and peppers, in 1441 Nuno Tristao and Antao Goncales captured 12 Africans and brought them back to Portugal, thus beginning the African slave trade. That the horrors of this undertaking actually were perceived as being carried out in the name of "our Lord God" was documented most acutely by a contemporary of the times, who described the capture of 165 Africans by a "Captain Lanzrate" in 1444.

> Our men, crying out "Sant' Iago! San Jorge! Portugal!" fell upon them killing or capturing all they could. There you might

> have seen mothers catch up their children, husbands their wives, each one escaping as best he could. Some plunged into the sea; others thought to hide themselves in the corners of their hovels; others hid their children under the shrubs . . . where our men found them. And at last our Lord God, Who gives to all a due reward, gave to our men that day a victory over their enemies; and in recompense for all their toil in His service, they took 165 men, women, and children, not counting the slain. (Foner, 1975, p. 97)

Because it was viewed as a means of saving the souls of heathens, the slave trade had the blessing of the church and rapidly became a regular part of Portuguese commerce. Soon Portugal began exporting slaves to Spain, and by the late 1500s, Africans were a sizable portion of both countries, often outnumbering Whites in some sections. However, one should not assume that the usual method of obtaining African slaves was to seize them in the manner of Tristao, Goncales, and Lanzrate. The African kings and the elite of the West African states were too powerful to be conquered by Europeans and were not conquered until after the slave trade was ended (Foner, 1975; Burkey, 1978). Therefore, it was only with the permission of the African kings that Europeans built forts on the Coast of Africa. The land on which the forts were built was rented and the types of materials used in building the forts sometimes were detailed by these kings.

As a consequence of the changing economy of Europe during the 1500s, with its developing focus on mercantile establishments, banking houses, and shipyards, there was a continuing reduction in the need for slaves. However, the discovery of America created a new demand, and by 1502, Black slaves were being forced to work in the mines of Santo Domingo, which originally was called Hispaniola and contained what is now Haiti and the Dominican Republic. In 1519, Charles the Great gave permission for the importing of 4,000 slaves per year to Hispaniola, Cuba, Jamaica, and Puerto Rico. The English did not enter the slave trade until 1562, when John Hawkins brought 300 Black slaves to Hispaniola, and most historians agree that it was not until August 1619 that slaves were introduced to what is now known as the United States. The 20 Africans brought here at that time, however, were not slaves but bondsmen and were designated in the court lists simply as servants, the same category that identified other indentured servants (Rolf, cited in Herskovits, 1935).

The number of slaves brought to the New World was quite large, and some authorities argue that as many as 70,000 per year were brought to the American colonies between 1716 and 1756. This would represent nearly three million slaves during that 41-year period. The same per annum figures are given for the years 1766 to 1800, a 25-year period. When we consider that the slave trade was in existence legally in the United States for almost 200 years (it was abolished here in 1808) and continued illegally for an unknown period after that, the probable number of Africans actually brought into the country becomes staggering. The figures for the French and Spanish colonies are similarly mind-boggling. An even greater agony is the recognition that the number imported represents only a portion of the people actually taken out of Africa, in view of the physically and mentally deleterious conditions under which slaves were held while awaiting "shipment" and the manner in which they were "packed" for passage. W.E.B. DuBois, (cited in Burkey, 1978) estimated that the total number of Blacks taken from Africa to the New World was approximately 15 million, while "other writers have accepted 15 million as the minimal amount with the probable total as 50 million; others have believed it was even higher than this" (Burkey, 1978, p. 187). As Foner points out (1975), "The general rule in the slave trade was that successful delivery of one-third of the cargo was enough to cover the total cost of the entire expedition with a 200 or 300 percent profit" (p. 120). Hence, slaves usually were tightly packed in order to increase profits. Described by Foner, the horrendously inhumane physical and psychological conditions on these ships were almost beyond belief. Very little space was reserved for supplies, because most had to be restricted for the "packing" of the "cargo" who were chained together in rows "sometimes with as little as eighteen inches between the floor and the ceiling" and "sometimes they were even forced to sit in each other's laps" (Foner, 1975, p. 120).

Because of the cramped conditions, the foul air, the accumulated human excreta, the poor food, the lack of water, and so on, there was much sickness and death on most slave ships. "There are records of captains who did not bother to clean up the accumulated filth, leaving their slaves to lie in their own excreta until the voyage was over" (Foner, 1975, p. 121). That the voyage from western Africa to the Americas lasted from six to ten weeks (and as long as four months from eastern Africa) intensifies the picture of almost unbelievable horror. Often, slaves committed suicide by refusing to eat or by tossing themselves into the sea. Others, because of illness and other reasons, were tossed into the sea by the crew.

The Source and Types of Africans Sold into Slavery

There is much evidence that the vast majority of slaves came from West Africa: the Northwestern Congo, the Gold Coast, the mouth of the Niger River, and so forth. Those slaves who were captured in the eastern part of the continent or in the interior of West Africa usually were taken to North Africa, Egypt, or Arabia, because it was too dangerous to take them over land to the West Coast.

In contrast with a widely-held belief, there is no evidence that those Africans who were sold into slavery were an inferior group or came from the least able elements of the African population. Investigation shows that the African slaves sent to the New World represented all classes and all strata of African society. This is quite understandable when we consider the sociopolitical structure of the early West African kingdoms and their methods of obtaining slaves, who in turn were sold to the Europeans. These kingdoms acquired most of their captives from two main types of warfare, in addition to the debtors and convicted lawbreakers: intergroup warfare and intragroup warfare. In obtaining slaves through intergroup warfare, all members of the enemy's group were subject to capture, whether they were men, women, children, or royalty. In intragroup warfare (the consequence of a rivalry among the contenders to a throne) the defeated contender, if not executed, was sold into slavery. Not only was the defeated challenger sold to the slavers, but so also were his family, all of their sympathizers, and the families of the sympathizers. Because the overwhelming numbers of captives were obtained from these two types of warfare, it is curious that some scholars, contrary to evidence, have focused on the convicted lawbreakers as the main source of slaves. As Foner (1975) points out, it would be well for Arthur R. Jensen of the University of California to study the nature of the slave trade before he claims, as he does, that the selection of slaves for docility and strength rather than for mental ability is the cause of present-day intellectual inferiority among African Americans.

The capturing of the slave was the first stage of the African's journey to the New World. The second stage, the "middle passage," involved the voyage across the Atlantic Ocean. Once in the New World, the African natives were sold on the auction block and transported to the plantations of the buyers, thus concluding the final stage of the journey. On the plantation, the Africans were ushered through a process that was designed to break their spirit and to produce the docile and hardworking animal that the Whites desired. Then the African became a unique and valuable source of uncompensated labor (Herskovits, 1935).

Before Africans were forced into slavery in North America, Indians and later Whites were tried as involuntary bondsmen. However, the Indians escaped into the forests and the Whites escaped and assimilated into normal society. Additionally, both groups were unable to withstand the heat and rigors of labor on the plantations. Thus, the use of Africans seemed to be more efficient and practical, and they were relegated to the task of developing the American economy through forced toil. Later, numerous rationalizations were advanced to justify the enslavement of millions of human beings, and the doctrine of inferiority developed as the major vindication. This myth has been so pervasive and so deeply rooted that it exists currently as the central core of present-day White racism (Comer, 1972).

Although the free Blacks enjoyed an enhanced social status, the development of North American slavery saw the beginnings of functional class distinctions among the enslaved. As miscegenation between the White master and the female slaves increased, the offspring of such unions frequently were assigned less rigorous and more desirable chores. Thus, a division of labor was instituted among the slaves by the slave master, and the embryonic manifestations of a Black class distinction began to emerge, mostly in the guises of field servants and house servants. The house servants not only enjoyed enhanced status by virtue of their privileged role and White ancestry, but also often were able to use their household skills as a means of earning manumission. This, in turn, elevated their status even higher. In contrast with the house servants

> Black field hands, who either attempted to hold onto the rudiments of a rapidly disappearing culture or who desperately tried to accommodate to the sketches of a new white culture, were forced to become America's underclassed—the lumpenproletariat of society. Primarily unskilled and untrained, they worked with their hands, engaged in menial tasks and supplied the brawn and labor necessary to build many of the physical structures of the American Republic. They suffered the abuse of low status and low esteem. They were forced to internalize white perceptions of their values and to deny the worth of their color. Thus, slavery produced a two-fold class system among Black Americans: an upper class based almost exclusively upon color and a lower class that consisted primarily of the sons and daughters of field hands. (Blackwell, 1985, p. 69)

Obviously, the masses of slaves were field servants, and the descendants of this group are those who constitute the masses of Blacks in this country.

The Experiences of Other Ethnic Groups in the United States

Although Blacks obviously are not the only ethnic group or minority in the United States, their historical position, and hence their accumulated experiences, have been quite different from those of other groups, although similar to some.

The major distinction is that the other groups, except for the indentured servants from European prisons, came to the New World voluntarily, seeking a better life with greater freedom and an enhancement of opportunities. Blacks, by contrast, arrived as a function of having been stripped of the very ideal that the other groups so desperately sought. The transplanted are viewed often as races or nationalities, but they should be seen more accurately as ethnic groups. Using a combination of definitions suggested by Gordon (1964), Rose (1964), and Mindel and Haberstein (1976), an ethnic group, for the purpose of the current discussion, is defined as a group of people who share a unique social and cultural heritage that is passed on from generation to generation as a function of race, religion, national origin, or some combination of these categories. On the other hand, a minority is "a group of people who, because of their physical or cultural characteristics, are singled out from the others in the society in which they live, for differential and unequal treatment, and who therefore regard themselves as objects of collective discrimination" (Wirth, cited in Mindel & Haberstein, 1976 p. 17).

In relation to the immigrant groups' responses to the New World culture, the concepts of "melting pot" and "cultural pluralism" have been advanced. The former term was introduced by Israel Zangwill in the title of his 1906 play (Mindel & Haberstein, 1976). The term suggests that the world's immigrants form a fusion here in the United States, thereby producing a new and perhaps even better amalgamation. The notion of cultural pluralism, on the other hand, was first presented in 1915 by Horace Kallen and implies that an immigrant group can become "American" while still maintaining its cultural heritage. A third view, "Anglo conformity," holds that the dominant Anglo culture subordinates and eliminates immigrant ethnicity and thereby places the Anglo culture in dominance (Mindel & Haberstein, 1976). In other words, the immigrant is "detribalized," "de-ethnicized," and finally "anglocized." But spawned by the civil rights movement of the 1960s and early 1970s, there has developed in the United States an increasing ethnic awareness and a resulting repudiation of Anglo conformity and melting-pot views.

The brief sketch that follows shows how the experiences of a few other ethnic groups contrast, historically, with those of Blacks and why the situation of the Black American is so unique. Most of the material presented here regarding those groups was taken from the work of Mindel and Haberstein (1976), with a significant portion concerning the Jews abstracted from Silberman (1985).

Italian Americans

Most Italian immigrants came to the United States from Southern Italy, Sicily, Corsica, and Sardinia. The largest number arrived between 1900 and 1914, when over three million immigrated. Because many planned to return to their homeland, they sought jobs that did not require long-term investments. Being mostly Catholic, they initially identified with the Irish Catholics when they arrived on these shores, but they soon recognized that the Irish had developed attitudes towards all foreigners that were as negative as those of other Americans. The Irish Americans, who already had been in the United States for several generations, felt that they had nothing in common with these lower-class, illiterate newcomers. The Italians' religious style was a particular source of criticism, and the competition with the Irish for jobs in the construction trades added additional tension. Because of this rejection by their fellow Catholics (their only potential allies in the New World), the Italians reestablished their village life and family patterns, and they added hundreds of social and direct-help societies. They highly valued family and kinship ties and found dignity in physical, manual labor: digging ditches, carrying garbage, sweeping streets, etc. Whenever possible, they would send money to relatives who had been left behind in Italy.

Because work, with its immediately necessary compensation, was valued over education and its delayed rewards, the Italian gravitated to blue-collar occupations rather than white-collar pursuits. This orientation seems to have had an impact even on present-day college students of Italian descent. Gottlieb and Sibbison (cited in Mindel & Haberstein, 1976) asked male and female Italian-American college students to explain their reasons for attending college and found that "job training" was the dominant reason, with abstract reasons such as "seeking knowledge" being subordinate.

Polish Americans

The Polish were among the last immigrants to come from Europe before the immigration acts of 1924, which finally limited Polish entrants to 6,488 per year. Tracing the beginning of their arrival to these shores, we find that artisans and adventurers came between 1608 and 1766; soldiers, writers, and noblemen came between 1766 and 1865; while peasants and landless farmers arrived between 1865 and 1929, when the 1924 immigration act became effective. The greatest migration from Poland was from 1900 to 1920 and the greatest single year was 1912–1913, when 174,365 entered the U.S. Most settled in industrial areas such as Chicago and Detroit, or in Pennsylvania mining towns such as Scranton and Erie. Very few went south or west. Like other groups that came to the United States, most of the Polish arrivals were part of the lower classes in the mother country. However, characteristics that distinguished them from members of the dominant culture, such as dress, manner of walk, and facial expression, were modifiable and even could be discarded altogether. Being unable to reproduce the structure and way of life of the homeland, the Polish people reformulated their culture in relation to the new environment. Also, because of the perceived hostility of the dominant culture, they tended to huddle together in subcommunities, particularly in urban locations. Importantly, rather than expecting to become Americanized, this group planned to earn money in the United States and then return to Poland. This provided further insulation against amalgamation.

Chinese Americans

Chinese immigration to the United States began with 42 new arrivals in 1853 and reached 117,000 by 1876. However, they were responded to very negatively by other Americans. One author in 1856 described them as having a physical appearance "designed to make people wonder that nature and custom should so combine to manufacture so much ugliness" (Huang, cited in Mindel & Haberstein, 1976, p. 124–125). Huang also referred to the Chinese women as "the most degraded and beastly of all human creatures." One anti-Chinese group, the Order of Caucasians, undertook the systematic murder of Chinese in order to protect Whites from total ruin. The Chinese were referred to as "chinks" and "yellow lepers," and they were burlesqued on Broadway as well as in the movies.

They initially came as laborers, having been invited to the United States by railroad agents who went to China and recruited them, promising plentiful work, high wages, and free passage. Because of the competition with White railroad workers and mine workers, the Chinese began to enter occupations that other immigrants tended to avoid, such as domestic service. Once they left the railroads and mines, they moved to the low-rent districts of the cities. This movement to the cities at first was due to discrimination and later was caused by an attempt to insulate themselves and provide mutual protection from a hostile world.

In a study of one large Chinese-American community, one investigator (Yuan, cited in Mindel & Haberstein, 1976) has suggested a four-stage developmental process to explain the progression of the Chinese from isolation to integration. According to Yuan, initially there was a closely knit ghettoization caused by the larger society's prejudice and hostility. Next, there was defensive insulation, because of the need for cooperation and mutual help against a hostile world. The third stage saw voluntary segregation accompanied by a strong sense of group identification. And the final stage was one of gradual assimilation into the larger society. This four-stage process may be applicable also to many of the other ethnic groups who migrated to these shores. It is interesting to note that the Chinese Exclusion Act of 1883 barred Chinese immigration altogether, and it was not until 1943 that the laws excluding them were repealed. The reasons for the change in negative attitudes towards the Chinese, as opposed to the persistently negative attitudes towards Blacks, should pose an important topic of investigation for the serious scholar.

Jewish Americans

A comprehensive account of the Jewish history on the United States is presented by Silberman (1985), and according to his portrayal, Jewish immigrants, in contrast with their persecution in many parts of Europe, found a relatively more hospitable environment in the New World. Since all of the early settlers were members of groups that came to America in search of religious freedom, Judaism found acceptance as merely an additional religious denomination. Jews, therefore, participated equally in the life of the community. By the time of the establishment of the Republic, American Jews were not distinguishable from other Americans, and they frequently intermarried with non-Jews.

However, between the 1820s and the 1850s, when Jews were forced out of central Europe because of anti-Semitism, the population of Jews in the United States increased from 3,000 to 150,000. Although many came from Vienna, Posen, and Alsace, the majority came from Bavaria and other parts of what later became the German Reich.

Those "German Jews" significantly altered the course of American Jewish life. Though at first regarded as being a "boisterous and earthy lot" whose close-to-the-surface emotions errupted with ease, the new immigrants soon began to acculturate and to disperse across the United States. Arriving during a period of both geographic and economic expansion, they became peddlars throughout the country. Peddling, being the chief means of transplanting city-made goods to the countryside, required little capital and no special skills, and it filled an economic need. As a result, German-Jewish immigrants quickly moved into the commercial middle-class in every part of the country, and they established synagogues wherever they went. By 1860, there were 160 Jewish communities from New York to San Francisco. However, these Jewish immigrants were not unique in moving up the economic ladder during this period of industrialization and rapid economic growth; for this was an era in the United States during which fortunes were being accumulated on a grand scale. Yet, Silberman tells us that:

> Even for this period, however, the Jewish ascent was remarkable; as the historian John Higham has written, no other immigrant group "has ever risen so rapidly from rags to riches." One-time peddlers became millionaires, among them investment bankers such as Joseph Seligman, Mayer Lehman, Marcus Goldman, and Solomon Loeb; retailers such as Benjamin Bloomingdale and Lazarus Straus; clothing manufacturers such as Levi Strauss and Philip Heidelbach; real estate brokers and developers such as Henry Morgenthau, Sr.; and the mining magnate Meyer Guggenheim. And affluence was not limited to this small elite; an 1890 Census Bureau survey of 10,000 Jewish families, most of them German immigrants, found that seven families in ten had at least one servant. (Silberman, 1985, p. 45)

However, one should be aware that the "second wave" of Jews who, after the assassination of Alexander II, arrived from Eastern Europe between 1881 and 1914, found an environment and a reception that were vastly different from those experienced by the earlier-arrived German Jews (Grayzel, 1947). Not only did the new arrivals face rejection by and friction with their more comfortably settled counterparts, but they also encountered further obstacles. Though coming from European environments that were primarily agricultural, they entered a New World that was becoming industrialized, whose cities were growing, and whose western frontiers were disappearing. Also complicating the picture was the sheer number of new arrivals. "Whereas there were only about 2,500 Jews in the country in 1899, 50,000 in 1850, and 250,000 in 1875, their numbers had risen to almost three millions by 1914" (Grayzel, 1947, p. 686).

As a consequence of these factors, the more recent immigrants found that, unlike the experience of the German Jews, peddling had become quite restricted and barely profitable. Thus, in order to earn a living, most sought employment in private industry; but many found themselves working in "sweatshops," earning unbelievably low wages and working 16 or more hours per day (Grayzel, 1947). These later arriving Jews, therefore, fell victim to a much greater poverty than was known to those who were part of the German Jewish migration.

The combination of the success of German Jews and the increased visibility of Eastern European Jews resulted in escalated anti-Jewish sentiment. The antidote for this anti-Semitism, according to many scholars, was for Jews to abandon their religion, customs, and anything that tended to distinguish them from others. This included redistributing Jews among businesses and professions to decrease overrepresentation and to increase underrepresentation. There also was a tendency to abandon the "chosen people" idea. Thus, expunging Jewishness meant avoiding the wearing of a yarmulke (traditional skullcap) in public, minimizing economic success, changing one's name, and even altering one's physical appearance. Interestingly, the surgical "nose job," which ostensibly transformed a "Jewish nose" into an "Anglo-Saxon nose," did not lose popularity until Barbara Streisand's rise to fame in the 1960s (Silberman, 1985). Silberman also reports that during the peak name-change period of the late 1940s and early 1950s, 80 percent of all applicants seeking to change their names were Jews. In underscoring the logic of such behavior, Silberman tells us of a cousin of his who had been turned down repeatedly for a job as an airline pilot, but who promptly was hired when he changed his name from Levy to Leeds. And an acquaintance was hired by the New York Telephone Company after changing her name from Prenowitz to Prentice.

The greatest journalist of this century, Walter Lippman strove to keep his Jewishness hidden and believed that: "The Jews are fairly distinct in their physical appearance and in the spelling of their names, from the run of the American people. They are, therefore, conspicuous" (cited in Silberman, 1985, p. 64). And it was this conspicuousness that was perceived to be the heart of the Jewish problem. Some even rejected their Jewishness altogether. One extreme example is that of Bernard Berenson, the Lithuanian-born art connoisseur and son of Jewish immigrants. Berenson was baptized as an Episcopalian at the age of twenty, later became a Catholic, spoke of himself as Anglo-Saxon, and eventually adopted anti-Semitism. It was not until the civil rights movement of the 1960s and 1970s, with its insistence on an open society, that publicly acknowledging one's Jewishness became increasingly widespread (Silberman, 1985).

Yet, Silberman tells us (p. 70) that Judaism defines itself as "an indelible status from which there is no exit." Furthermore, as a result of having been born into Judaism, all Jews are bound by the covenant delivered on Mount Sinai between God and the Jewish people. Thus, "one may be a good Jew or a bad Jew, a religious Jew or a secular Jew; one may even stop identifying oneself as a Jew; but one never stops being a Jew—even after conversion to another religion" (Silberman, 1985, p. 71). In fact, Silberman points out that the Catholic Archbishop of Paris, Cardinal Jean-Marie Lustiger, because he was born a Jew, has always considered himself to be Jewish. Being a Jew, then, is very different from being a Protestant or a Roman Catholic, because Judaism is determined by an involuntary commitment to a fate, rather than by the voluntary adoption of a set of beliefs or practices.

The current presence of cultural differences in the United States verifies that America never has been a "melting pot." Although the original cultures of the immigrants may have been modified by the New World experience, distinct cultures do still exist (Glazer & Moynihan, cited in Silberman, 1985). In fact, as Silberman tells us, the increased openness of society, as a consequence of the civil rights movement of the 1960s and 1970s, may have contributed to a strengthening of cultural bonds, since such openness not only tended to increase ethnic conspicuousness but also served to foster a need for the security that shared ethnicity provided.

The Uniqueness of the Black Situation

From this brief description of the early circumstances of several present-day ethnic groups in the United States, it becomes clear that the overall plight of Blacks has had a distinctly singular and virtually incomparable history. As pointed out by Staples (1976), four traits distinguish Blacks from other ethnic groups who arrived on these shores: (1) Blacks came from a country with norms and values that were different from those of other immigrants; (2) The Blacks were composed of many different tribes, each with its own languages, cultures, and traditions; (3) In the beginning they came without females; and (4) Most importantly, they came in bondage. Both during and subsequent to slavery, African Americans not only were physically, mentally, and legally prevented from participating fully in American society but also were constrained in their efforts to learn even the fundamentals of standard communication. Slave codes prohibiting the teaching of literacy skills to Blacks, as well as the various segregation laws that were developed after emancipation, created a degree of second-class citizenship unlike that experienced by any other ethnic group. Even the "indelible status" of the Jew cannot be compared with the ineffaceability of racial identity that is occasioned by one's Blackness. A name change or "nose job," even when supplemented by other attempts at physical alteration (such as hair-straightening and skin-lightening), would be of questionable effectiveness for Africans who desire to escape from or to conceal their racial identity.

African Survivals

A persistent question that seems to escape a definite answer relates to the degree to which elements of African culture were retained after the Africans entered the New World. Burkey (1978), while taking the position that during slavery most of the African heritage was lost because of the "resocialization" and "deculturation" processes, points out several elements that were retained. The culturally deleterious practices of separating family members by selling them to different plantations, socializing the slave children into rudiments of Eurocentric culture, and the persistent desire of missionaries and Anglo church groups to Christianize the Africans, reduced the likelihood of imparting African heritage to the slave children; and this restricted likelihood became more attenuated with each generation.

One of the African's most enduring survivals in the New World is represented by the structure, content, and practice of Black religion. The roots of current Black American religion are in Africa, but some of the branches were transplanted to the Americas during the slave trade. In spite of the wide variety of religious forms that existed in Africa during the slave trade and still exist today, commonality may be found in the belief in and interaction between religion and one's daily life, a belief in animism, and a belief in ancestral spirits who become gods and look after the family subsequent to death (Staples, 1976).

One result of the intergroup and intragroup wars in Africa and the capture of a wide cross section of the African population was that a highly disproportionate number of priests were among those sold to the Europeans for eventual transfer to the Americas, the Caribbean, and South America. The reason for this was that when a conquest was made as a result of warfare, the highly-trained priests not only were among the most intransigent of the conquered, but also were the most dangerous to the conquerors. With their ability to call upon their indignant gods, these revered priests could ferment unrest among their followers. Thus, selling a priest to the European slavers was a convenient method for a victor to break the spirit of an overthrown group of rivals or a tribe captured in warfare (Herskovits, 1935). The New World slaves, therefore, brought with them both their religion and a heavy concentration of religious leaders. When Christianity later was taught to the slaves, they attempted to fuse it with the rudiments of their African heritage, and the Black church was born (Frazier, 1964). This church as an institution initially was invisible structurally, but it was quite real functionally and stressed the glories of the "afterworld" as a means of reducing the impact of the oppressed condition. Significantly, the attractiveness and popularity of the spiritual hymn, with its resemblance to the African shout songs, may have been due to the emotional-expressive and tension-release quality of the music and lyrics.

As has been pointed out by Lewis (1955), the Black church gave and still gives its members the sorts of religious experiences that provide strength and a feeling of group cohesiveness that are enhanced by the African-derived chant-response interaction between minister and congregation. This type of interactional response is found most prominently in Black American music and forms the basis for spirituals and moaning hymns, the two oldest forms of pure Black American music (Jordan, 1975). This call-response style also is quite observable in the way in which the Black minister and his audience engage in ongoing emotional release (Smitherman, 1977). The present author recalls his childhood when he sat in awe at the emotional stimulation and virtual magic of this method of interaction. The responses of the congregation would be delivered not in unison but with individual creativity and apparently unpredictable timing. Much of it appeared to be similar to the variety of responses one hears from the spectators at a baseball game when the star pitcher is delivering a series of strikes. Indeed, the carefully chosen words of the minister seem to be so timed as to encourage this very effect. He speaks a few words of a sentence, pauses for the response, and then continues for another few words, pauses for another response, etc. This unique style of interaction, though most noticeable in the Black church, can be found in virtually all other aspects of Black culture that depend upon interpersonal communication. This matter will be discussed in somewhat more detail in chapter 10.

Because, in Africa, the training of the priest touched upon the functions of many other specialists, including those of medicine man and witch doctor (Mbiti, 1969), the Black minister in the United States became "the interpreter of the unknown, the healer of the sick, the supernatural avenger of wrong, and the one individual who expressed the longing, disappointment and resentment of a stolen and oppressed people" (Staples, 1976, p. 158). Furthermore, "during slavery, the church was the one place Ole Massa allowed the slaves to congregate unsupervised and to do pretty nearly as they pleased. Not surprisingly, a number of slave rebellions and revolutionary leaders (such as Preacher Nat Turner) were spawned in the church" (Smitherman, 1977, p. 90).

A brief history of the Black American church subsequent to slavery indicates that:

> The first Black church as an organization was founded in Philadelphia in 1794 after a discriminatory incident. Prayers were interrupted in the St. George Methodist Episcopal Church to make several black leaders leave their seats and sit in the gallery. One of these men formed the all-Black St. Thomas Protestant Episcopal Church. Two years later, in New York City, the African Methodist Episcopal Zion Church was organized, which then spread to other cities. The second major church, the Colored Methodist Episcopal Church, was founded after the Civil War, and numerous Black Baptist churches also gained in popularity. By 1900, there were 2.7 million church members in a black population of 8.3 million. The black church not only provided a place of worship free from White dominance and hostility, but also carried on education and provided a training ground for Black leaders. The Black church founded schools and colleges in the South, and was important in forming secular mutual aide organizations, such as insurance companies, burial societies, and lodges. In the words of the Black sociologist E. Franklin Frazier, the church was the Negro's "refuge in a hostile White world. (Burkey, 1978, p. 268)

Clark (1965) has indicated that the Black church provides Blacks with a means of compensating for the subordination, restrictions, and general wretchedness under which they are forced to live, and has furnished the only basis for esteem. He indicates further that, in addition to the cathartic role, the Black church serves as a recreational club and as a means of status-elevation where maids and porters are able to counterbalance their subordinate roles in the larger society.

The mental health aspect of this status elevation is underscored when we consider that:

> The traditional Black church is peopled by working class Blacks—domestics, factory workers, janitors, unskilled laborers. While today there is an ever-increasing number of high school graduates and college-educated members, most "Pillars of the Church" have less than a high school education. The preacher of such a church may or may not be university-educated, but he must be able to "talk that talk" (preach in Black English style and lingo). It is within the traditional Black church that traditional Black folk (Blacks who haven't been assimilated into the elusive American mainstream) create much of their reality, which includes the preservation and passing on of Africanized idioms, proverbs, customs, and attitudes. (Smitherman, 1977, p. 90)

Staples (1976) has shown that in addition to the functions of compensation, strengthening identity, and assisting in the release of emotional tension, the Black church has been instrumental in maintaining family solidarity, developing leadership, serving as a center for Black protest, and providing for general social interaction. Amplifying this social function, Smitherman reminds us that "since the traditional Black church is a social as well as a religious unit, the preacher's job as leader of his flock is to make churchgoers feel at home and to deal with the problems and realities confronting his people as they cope with the demands and stresses of daily living. Thus, preachers are given wide latitude as to the topics they can discuss and the methods of presentation" (p. 87).

Concept of Time

Another Africanism which seems to have survived is the concept of duration, interlude, and the occasion of events. Many informal observers have recognized that the concept of time seems to be regarded differently by Blacks as compared to Whites, not only in the United States but also throughout the diaspora. Western visitors to the various islands of the Caribbean complained that buses seldom are "on time," and in the United States the concept of "C.P. Time" is a constant reminder of the Black-White cultural difference in the conceptualization of time. However, like language, this difference often has been looked upon as being another manifestation of the universality of Black cultural inferiority, thereby strengthening the laziness-shiftlessness myth and italicizing Dobzhansky's observation (1973) that we tend to ascribe deficits to differences.

According to the *Encyclopaedia Britannica* (1972), time "is a basic concept that deals with the occurrence of events. There is a definite order in which any two simultaneous events occur at some location. If A and B are such events, either A occurs before B or B occurs before A. Between two nonsimultaneous occurrences, there is a lapse of an interval of time. The measurement of time involves establishing a precise system of reference for specifying when any event occurs; that is, specifying the epoch and establishing a standard interval of time" (vol. 21, p. 1155). The reference scales used by most peoples of the world are the rotation of the earth about its axis, which takes 24 hours to complete, and the rotation of the earth about the sun, which is approximately 365 days in duration. The mathematically determined multiples and subdivisions of these rotations (years, months, days, hours, etc.) are referred to collectively as "time."

However, the African-American concept of time cannot be understood unless it is seen within the religious ontology of African life and viewed as a vestige of African culture that has survived the obliterating effects of Western influence. There is virtually no literature on this subject, but Mbiti (1969) provides us with enough information to illuminate the African connection. According to his research, African time consists of events: those which have occurred already (past), those which currently are transpiring (present), and those which are to take place immediately (immediate future). An absence of time constitutes those events which either have not occurred or are not likely to occur immediately. But African time is essentially bidimensional: past and present, with only a small degree of future. The distant future is, for the African, an almost incomprehensible concept, because the events signifying its existence have not taken place. Even the *immediate* future indicates only potential time and technically lies external to the realm of actual time. In African langauges, the future tense of verbs extend only to two years, and some of these languages restrict the future tense to only six months. Hence, for the Africans, time is a series of events, and Mbiti (1969) tells us that

> an expectant mother counts the lunar months of her pregnancy; a traveller counts the number of days it takes him to walk (in former years) from one part of the country to another. The day, the month, the year, one's life time or human history,

> are all divided up or reckoned according to their specific events, for it is these that make them meaningful. For example, the rising of the sun is an event which is recognized by the whole community. It does not matter, therefore, whether the sun rises at 5 a.m. or 7 a.m., so long as it rises. When a person says that he will meet another at sunrise, it does not matter whether the meeing takes place at 5 a.m. or 7 a.m., so long as it is during the general period of sunrise. Likewise, it does not matter whether people go to bed at 9 p.m. or at 12 midnight; the important thing is the event of going to bed, and it is immaterial whether in one night this takes place at 10 p.m. while in another it is at midnight. For the people concerned, time is meaningful at the point of the *event* [italics mine] and not at the mathematical moment. (P. 19)

Hence the Caribbean bus leaves the point of origin in the *event* that a reasonable number of passengers have boarded. Informal observations by this author indicate that the bus passengers and awaiting passengers tend to accept this situation as being normal.

In contrast with African time, Eurocentric time is based on only one event; namely, the rotation of the earth. Therefore, the New York City bus leaves the point of debarkation in the event that the earth has rotated to a given position. This fundamental difference in the perception of time sets the stage for a wide range of Black-White behavioral differences in matters relating to temporal consistency, punctuality, and so on. Assigning an European value to the difference seems to suggest, as usual, that the African concept is inferior, simply because it is of limited adaptability in the larger society, which is geared rigidly to rotational time as the only referent. Other African survivals that have been mentioned by various scholars, in addition to language, are communication styles, music, and art (Mbiti, 1969; Baratz, 1971; Nobles, 1972; Smitherman, 1977). Another survival, interpersonalism (as opposed to the Eurocentric individualism) appears to be especially relevant to Africans throughout the diaspora and will be discussed in chapter 6.

CHAPTER TWO

Black Psychology and Black Psychologists

Defining Black Psychology

Recognizing that psychological principles deal with the organism's response to physical and nonphysical stimuli, most psychologists agree that psychology involves the study of the behavior and mental processes of living organisms. However, mental processes may be absent in many forms of life and in other forms such processes usually are not directly accessible. Hence, although psychology has been defined as involving both behavior and mental phenomena (English & English, 1958; Chaplin, 1975), it must be recognized that what we study directly is behavior and that from the behavior we merely draw inferences about the underlying processes (Darley et al., 1984). Because behavioral responses presuppose a stimulus, psychological concepts and models, in the final analysis, tend to deal with the relationships among the stimulus or stimulus situation, the consequent response of the organism, and any mediating factors. It is critical to acknowledge, then, that human beings of African origin, as a group, have experienced and still are experiencing a common core of stimuli that differ qualitatively and quantitatively from those of other peoples of the world. The shared experiences result in a commonality of experience and mediation results in ethnically distinct behavior, as the organism constantly adjusts to the perceived world. The cumulative effect of the resultant overt and covert behavior produces values, standards, customs, and traditions that eventually become racially singular. This uniqueness becomes manifest in learning, perception, motivation, personality development, and an overall world view that serves to differentiate between the psychological characteristics of the displaced African and those of the larger culture. These considerations are not intended to suggest that there is intra-group *uniformity* or an absence of diversity among members of the supplanted African subculture. Rather, the implication is in the direction of a *common core*. In recognition of this common nucleus and the resulting inapplicability of many Eurocentric theories to Black people, there is a growing belief among many Black psychologists that in the United States the developing discipline of Black psychology must take into consideration African philosophy, African traditions, and the African–New World experience. Most of the theory of this new discipline will have to be developed by Black scholars and scientists. However, as pointed out by Baldwin (1976), some Black psychologists believe that a functional definition of Black psychology, though undeniably focused on objective analysis of Black behavior, may involve other than Black scientists and researchers, so long as the analytical base is Africentric. The present author believes it to be most improbable that a researcher who is not imbued with Black culture would have the perceptions, psychological sets, and other predispositions that would allow for Africentric interpretation of data. Yet, we should be careful to avoid throwing out the baby with the bath water. It very well may be that the *interpretations* offered and the *conclusions* drawn, rather than the principles and theories themselves, are at the heart of the negative, deficient, pathological picture that Eurocentric research paints of Black people.

Thus, it is possible that some of the existing principles and theories, with modification, may be helpful in understanding and enhancing the Black experience. For example, thoroughly understanding the development of effective and ineffective Black coping behavior may be facilitated by an understanding not only of African genesis but also of current information on operant conditioning, classical conditioning, and social learning theory. In like manner, an understanding of Black belief systems might be facilitated by an examination of the existing principles of perception and consciousness. But much of the theory and methodology of Black psychology is yet to be developed. Because this unfolding seems to require an Africentric actuation, the task of the Black humanist and behavioral scientist is formidable but unclouded: to develop theories and a methodology for the scientific study of the behavior and consciousness of people of African heritage, with a view towards improving their life conditions. Rather than resurrect in Black trappings the age-old polemic concerning the nature of psychology (behavior or consciousness), the Black psychologist should be mindful that the inclusion of consciousness is critical to our mission, in view of the West African belief in a synchronous relationship between consciousness and behavior.

For example, Nobles (1972) tells us that in West African society there was no separation between belief and action, since both belonged to a single whole. Hence, "what people do is motivated by what they believe, and what they believe springs from what they do and experience." (Mbiti, cited in Nobles, 1972). Accordingly, Black psychology should concern itself with both behavior and consciousness, acknowledging that attention to the one and subordination of the other sometimes may be required.

Black American Psychologists

While most psychologists regard the year 1879, when Wilhelm Wundt established his laboratory in Germany, as the beginnng of scientific psychology, and trace their roots to British, German, and Greek philosophy, Black American psychologists should trace their origins to Africa and the United States. The many shamans, tribal healers, rainmakers, and witch doctors in the motherland doubtlessly contributed to both the understanding and the shaping of our ancestors' beliefs, attitudes, emotions, and behavior. Although the extent to which these African influences survived in the New World is arguable, it is clear that the present humanistic focus of American Black psychology evolved from the general training and thrust of early Black psychologists in the United States, who in turn reflected an African interpersonalism. Hence, it is not surprising to learn that prior to 1941 psychology courses in many predominantly Black institutions were found only in departments of education, thus minimizing the scientific-laboratory focus of the White establishment. It also is no marvel that the undisputed father of American Black psychology, Dr. Francis Cecil Sumner, was primarily a humanist, rather than a brass instrument, laboratory-experimentalist (Guthrie, 1976).

Prior to 1920, only eleven Blacks had earned the Ph.D. in the United States, throughout all disciplines, although a total of 10,000 such degrees had been awarded. The very first Black to receive the Ph.D. in any discipline in the United States was Edward Bouchet, who in 1876 earned that degree in physics at Yale University. Concerning the first (White) American Ph.D. in psychology, there seems to be some controversy. Guthrie (1976) gives this distinction to Joseph Jastrow, who studied under G. Stanley Hall at Johns Hopkins University and was awarded the Ph.D. in 1886. However, Harvard claims to have awarded the first psychology doctorate to G. Stanley Hall in 1878 (Harper, 1949). Remarking on this matter, Harper states:

> It is a nice question as to whether there were American doctorates in psychology before 1884. Harvard begins its list with G. Stanley Hall in 1878. He wrote a dissertation on the perception of space "in H. P. Bowditch's laboratory" under the direction of William James. (Harvard's first Ph.D. was given in 1873 and Hall's was its eighteenth, but the first in the Department of Philosophy as well as in the field of Psychology. The first earned Ph.D. to be granted in America in any subject was conferred by Yale in 1861. Pennsylvania became, in 1870, the second American university to confer the doctorate, and three years later, Harvard became the third university to grant an earned Ph.D.). After Hall's degree, all the doctorates in psychology were given under Hall at Hopkins and then at Clark until 1893, when C. W. Miller received his at Pennsylvania and C. B. Bliss and E. F. Buchner theirs at Yale. Jastrow claimed that he received the first Ph.D. in bona fide psychology in 1886 at Hopkins, that Hall's (1878) at Harvard and John Dewey's (1884) and M. I. Swift's (1885) were not experimental and belonged to the philosophical tradition. (P. 585)

However, there is no question that the first Black American to earn the doctorate in psychology was Francis Cecil Sumner, who received the Ph.D. in 1920 from Clark University in Massachusetts, under the supervision of G. Stanley Hall (Guthrie, 1976). Dr. Sumner was born on December 7, 1895, in Pine Bluff, Arkansas. After completing his studies at Clark, he taught at Wilberforce University in Ohio, Southern University in Louisiana, West Virginia State College, and finally Howard University in Washington, D.C., where he was chairperson of the psychology department from 1928 until his death in 1954 at the age of 59. At Howard, Dr. Sumner established a strong department which, although he was a humanist, had a laboratory-experimental component, in keeping with the emphasis of most White colleges and in contrast with the teacher-training focalization of most other Black institutions. Between 1919 and 1938, Howard University was the nation's only predominantly Black educational institution with a graduate program in psychology (Guthrie, 1976, p. 10). Although he was interested mainly in creating a first-rate psychology department and in preparing students for entry into doctoral programs, Sumner was strongly interested in the psychology of religion. However, he directed much of his research efforts toward the understanding and elimination of racial bias in the administration of justice.

Five years after Sumner earned his degree at Clark, Dr. Charles Henry Thompson earned his Ph.D. in educational psychology at the University of Chicago. From 1926 until his death in 1975, Dr. Thompson served at Howard University as a faculty member and administrator. For over 30 years, he was the editor of the prestigious *Journal of Negro Education*. In 1933, Beverly Prosser earned the Ph.D. in educational psychology at the University of Cincinnati, thereby becoming the first Black female to earn the doctorate in psychology. From 1920 until 1935 a total of eight Blacks received doctorates in the field of psychology, with all but two having been awarded in educational psychology. During the subsequent 15 years, an additional 23 psychology doctorates were awarded to Blacks, but only five were in educational psychology. Although figures on the number of all American psychology doctorates awarded between 1920 and 1950 were not available, Harper's 1949 data showed that 2,528 such degrees were awarded between 1919 and 1948 (pp. 582–584). Thus it appears that the Black portion of the total pool of psychology doctorates from 1920 to 1950 probably was less than 1 percent.

Of the 32 doctorates awarded to Blacks during this 31-year period (1920–1950), nearly 50 percent were based on dissertations with titles reflecting an orientation towards Black concerns (Guthrie, 1976, pp. 125–127). Moreover, virtually all of these early psychologists, regardless of their dissertation topics, concentrated much of their research and/or professional activities on the understanding of, dispelling myths about, or enhancing the quality of the Black experience in the United States. These activities certainly isolated them from mainstream psychology (Boykin et al., 1979) which at that time was interested primarily in rigidly controlled laboratory experimentation, initially dealing with subjectively reported sensations and later with observable behavior.

Between 1951 and 1974, there apparently was no systematic accounting of Black doctorates in psychology, but the National Science Foundation has been keeping such figures since 1975. This information indicates that of the 21,225 psychology doctorates issued between 1975 and 1981, 706 (3.33 percent) were awarded to Blacks. Table 2.1 shows the Black-White distribution of these degrees for that seven-

TABLE 2.1

Clinical & Non-Clinical Psychology Doctorates Earned by Blacks and Whites From 1975 to 1981[a]

Speciality	*1975*	*1976*	*1977*	*1978*	*1979*	*1980*	*1981*	*Total*
				BLACKS				
Non Clinical	56	57	55	58	75	76	58	435
Clinical	22	29	40	42	40	43	55	271
Total	78	86	95	100	115	119	113	706
% Clinical	28.21	33.72	42.11	42.00	34.78	36.13	48.17	38.39
				WHITES				
Non Clinical	1885	1943	1999	1936	1947	1916	2943	13669
Clinical	788	854	896	1019	1029	1063	1201	6850
Total	2673	2797	2895	2955	2976	2979	3244	20519
% Clinical	29.48	30.53	30.95	34.48	34.58	35.68	37.02	33.38
Black + White	2751	2883	2990	3055	2091	3098	3357	21225
% Black	2.83	2.98	3.18	3.27	3.72	3.84	3.27	3.33

year period, including the proportions with the clinical specialization. There was a slight but steady increase in the proportion of Black recipients until 1981, when there was a slight decrease. In that same year, there was also a sharp rise in the percentage of Blacks who earned their degrees in clinical psychology. Whether both of these changes may have been a function of a third factor, such as economic conservatism, might be a question for further research. When the Black percentage of 3.33 percent for the years 1975 to 1981 is compared with the approximately one percent for the years 1920 to 1950, it becomes clear that at this rate we will be well into the twenty-first century before Blacks constitute even five percent of psychology doctorates. Although we do not have the figures as yet, Boykin et al. (1979) tells us that the acceleration in doctoral level Black psychologists coincided with the heightened social legislation of the 1960s and 1970s and its demand for increased psychological services. One result was an enhancement of opportunities for Blacks within the field of psychology. Also, the burgeoning civil rights movement caused many of these psychologists to recognize the need for increased numbers and elevated professional involvement in the Black struggle. Many of them felt that this goal could not be facilitated and might even be hindered by continuation of active membership in White-dominated organizations, such as the American Psychological Association. There was the additional feeling that much of the racism of psychiatry (Thomas & Sillen, 1972) was also characteristic of psychology, particularly in the institutionalized sense. Others felt that even if professional psychology in general were not actually racist, its major organization was nevertheless elitist, relatively conservative, insensitive to the needs of minorities, and hence irrelevant for Black psychologists. Consequently, in 1968, in San Francisco, California, the Association of Black Psychologists (ABPsi) was born. Concerning the history and present status of this organization, the 1984–85 information brochure states that:

> Guided by the principle of self-determination, these Black psychologists set about building an institution through which they could address the long neglected needs of Black professionals and begin to impact positively upon the mental health of the national Black community by means of planning programs, services, training, and advocacy.
>
> The Founding Members originally committed themselves to:
>
> 1. Organize their skills and abilities to influence and effect necessary change.

2. Address themselves to significant social problems affecting the Black community in particular, as well as other segments of population whose needs society has not fulfilled.

The Association of Black Psychologists has grown from a handful of concerned professionals into an independent, autonomous organization of over 600 members who are in the forefront in addressing issues of psychological nature which have adverse effects in our communities.

The Association is currently involved in two of the Congressional Black Caucus Brain Trusts in the area of Health and the Aged.

ABPsi's Organizational Goals

1. To enhance the psychological well-being of Black people in America.
2. To promote constructive understanding of Black people through positive approaches to research.
3. To develop an approach to psychology that is consistent with the experience of Black people.
4. To define mental health in consonance with newly established psychological concepts and standards regarding Black people.
5. To develop internal support systems for Black psychologists and students of psychology.
6. To develop policies for local, state and national decision making which impact on the mental health of the Black community.
7. To promote values and a life style that supports our survival and well-being as a race.
8. To support established Black organizations and aid in the development of new independent Black institutions to enhance our psychological, educational, cultural, and economic situation.

This association, which publishes among other things a newsletter and the *Journal of Black Psychology,* has a membership comprised of professionals, students, and other qualified persons who are interested in promoting its goals. Presently, the more than 600 members are located in 26 chapters throughout the United States, with headquarters in Washington, D.C.

As is indicated by a review of the entries in the latest Biographical Directory of this association (Black Psychologists Today, 1978), its members are engaged in a wide range of psychological endeavors but seem to be concentrated in the humanistic specialties (i.e., professional pursuits that are directly useful for the improvement of human life) rather than in the more positivistic, mechanistic undertakings. Because many Black psychologists are not affiliated professionally with ABPsi, it is not possible to generalize conclusively about the vocational orientations of most Black psychologists. However, informal discussions support the suggestion that there is a widespread heavy convergence towards humanistic pursuits. One highly acclaimed work on Black psychology (Jenkins, 1982) argues that for Black psychologists and for Black people in general, the humanistic approach has greater viability. As a result, we see Black and other minority psychologists who are critical of the rigid application of intelligence and specific aptitude test scores to the quest for achievement prediction, especially when cultural factors are ignored (Williams, 1972; Samuda, 1975; Boyd, 1977; Houston, 1980).

Because one aspect of Black psychology is behavioral and is concerned with the responses of Black people to their environment, it is possible that these responses and the precipitating stimuli can be studied in a manner that utilizes the scientific method. Just as a great deal of Black popular music, certainly different in quality from White popular music, can be written and studied by use of universally accepted symbols, so too much of Black behavior possibly may be assessed through the aid of generally accepted procedures of scientific inquiry. Pragmatically, some of these procedures may require modification, but others may have immediate applicability.

Traditional Methods of Studying Behavior

Over the years, psychology has recognized four basic methods of studying behavior: (1) the case history method, (2) the field study method (also called the method of naturalistic observation), (3) the survey method, and (4) the experimental method (Ruch, 1963; Darley et al., 1984). All of these approaches involve attempts to discern, in a systematic way, the relationship(s) between the stimulus situation and the response of the organism, and all tend to comply with the *scientific method.* Fundamental to this method is the requirement that the investigator deal only with factors that can be observed and measured. In addition, there is the stipulation that prescribed steps be followed in an established order. The first step is (a) to recognize that a problem exists; next is (b) the formulation of an hypothesis (an educated "guess" about the cause-effect relationship); then (c) a plan for collecting the data is developed followed by (d) the actual collection of the data. Subsequently, (e) the data must be analyzed and finally (f) the hypothesis is either accepted, rejected, or modified. The four methods of studying behavior, mentioned above, and somewhat amplified below, differ primarily in the plan and procedure for collecting the data.

In the *case history method,* the psychologist conducts an in-depth study of an individual's life in order to determine the cause or causes of a particular behavior. Sometimes the approach is biographical, where the researcher analyses a previously recorded history or behavior, and at other times it involves the compilation of a short history by exploring the present life situation of the subject. The *field study method,* often referred to as the *naturalistic observation method,* involves observations of naturally occurring events, without any experimental manipulation. In fact, the subjects may be completely unaware that they are being observed. In the *survey method,* the investigator collects data from a randomly selected group by means of oral interviews or a questionnaire. This is the method used by most public opinion polls. The most sophisticated technique is the *experimental method,* involving a highly developed procedure for isolating the variables and collecting the data. Because of such refinement, this method is regarded by most scientists as being superior to the other techniques. Central to this experimental approach is the systematic manner of isolating the variables. Variables are factors or conditions which are suspected of being crucial to the problem under investigation. They are called variables because they vary either qualitatively or quantitatively. For example, race could be a variable in a given investigation and might vary threefold (Black, White, and Asian) or only twofold (Black and White). In the same investigation, the score obtained on an intelligence test might be another variable, varying from possibly a low of 65 to a high of 146. (Note that intelligence *per se* cannot be measured directly with any currently known procedure.) Some of these variables, because they are dependent upon (caused by) antecedent factors, are referred to as *dependent variables.* Others, since they are the causal agents and hence "independent," are termed *independent variables.* Stated differently, the independent variable is similar to cause and the dependent variable is similar to effect. A third factor, the *intervening variable,* is a non-observed factor, a hypothetical construct, which serves to account for the relationship between the independent and dependent variables. For example, it may be observed that on a particular test the average score of Blacks is lower than the average score for Whites. Assuming that the test is valid, it may be concluded that a motivational factor is responsible for the racial difference in test score. In this case, the motivational factor would be an intervening variable or hypothetical construct, since it was not direclty observed or measured. Numerous conflicts and arguments in psychology are based on just such intervening variables rather than on actual experimental findings, many of which are noncontroversial. An example is the I.Q. controversy discussed in chapter 4. Black psychologists, including this author, agree that Blacks tend to earn lower scores than Whites on instruments that are labeled intelligence tests. The point of controversy is *why* the difference exists. Those who argue that it is due to a genetic factor are resorting to an intervening variable, since no one yet has measured the genetic factor. By the same logic the term "intelligence" itself is a hypothetical construct, while the score on the test (whatever it measures) is an observable and quantifiable factor.

Basic to the experimental method is prediction, and the experimenter usually predicts that, as a demonstration of a probable causal relationship, changes will occur in the dependent variable when changes are made in the independent variable. However, the predictable consequences of modifying the independent variable cannot be determined accurately unless there is containment and curbing of other possibly independent variables. The holding in check of variables which *could* be influential is known as *experimental control.* For example, suppose it was desired to know the effect of reprimand (independent variable) on the arithmetic performance of a group of subjects. To assess this problem, one could administer an arithmetic test to the subjects both prior and subsequent to reprimanding them, and then compare the scores under the two sets of conditions. In this example, the subjects serve as their own controls and there is little question as to whether one or more unwanted variables are operating differentially in the two situations, because the *same people* are used under each condition. Considering that the critical independent variable (reprimand) would be different under the two conditions (at first absent and subsequently present) it alone would appear to be responsible for any difference in score. In such an experiment, the scores would be expected to be lower after the reprimand than before. It is possible, however, that some personal variable might change from one condition to the other. As a result of the practice prior to reprimand, all subjects might improve in arithmetic ability and obtain *higher* scores after the reprimand, thereby causing the experimenter to draw the erroneous conclusion that the higher scores were related to the reprimand. In order to eliminate this problem, the experimenter might use two groups; one group would receive the reprimand (the experimental group) and the other would be treated normally and receive no reprimand (the control group). Both groups should be the same on all variables except reprimand, and both should be reacted to uniformly by the experimenter. Then any difference in arithmetic performance (the dependent variable) may be attributed to the sole difference that exists in the two levels of the independent variable (reprimand vs. no reprimand).

Once collected, the data must be evaluated in order to be meaningful. Since virtually all information gathered under the experimental method is quantitative, it becomes consequential only after it is analyzed mathematically. A discussion of the techniques and procedures for doing this is beyond the scope of this book, but clear explanations are given by Edwards (1974), Ferguson (1976), and Linton and Gallo (1975). The Linton and Gallo text is particularly recommended, because it gives also a good accounting of experimental methodology.

It is not suggested that for our purposes one of the four methods mentioned above is more relevant or in some way superior to the others. In fact, it may be that they all are universally applicable in varied situations and therefore helpful in obtaining valid information and establishing relative truths about Black people. As Georgia State Senator Julian Bond remarked at a lecture on the Douglass College campus of Rutgers University a few years ago, "If your house is on fire, and someone offers you a bucket of water, don't ask who he is, don't ask where he got it from, just make sure it is not gasoline and pour it on!"

CHAPTER THREE

Learning and Conditioning

> . . . while the experiences of Black people in this country are unique, the principles of psychological functioning are by definition universal. (Grier & Cobbs, cited in Guthrie, 1970, p. 182)

Learning has been defined as the acquisition of any relatively permanent change in behavior as a result of practice or experience (Chaplin, 1975), and this type of acquisition seems to explain much of human behavior. However, since the experiences of Blacks in the United States are essentially different from those of Whites, the content of the learning also would seem to be dissimilar. One major problem here is that the dominant group tends to explain the dissimilarities in terms of minority group characteristics rather than in terms of deficiencies in the social system. Thus, "despite the Kerner Report's unequivocal ascription of the major responsibility for the 'explosive' racial conditions in American cities to White racism, most White Americans still deny the role of external societal forces and agree that Blacks themselves are primarily responsible for the conditions in which they find themselves" (Yetman & Steele, 1971, p. 8). Many such conditions in which Blacks find themselves, and to which they respond in a predictable way, are caused by overt or covert learning situations.

Although several types of learning have been identified in the past, the types that seem to have received the most attention are the *classical conditioning theory* of the Russian physiologist Ivan P. Pavlov, the *operant conditioning theory* of America's B. F. Skinner, and (more recently) the *social learning theory* of America's Albert Bandura. There is no assumption that these three theories account for all or even most learned behavior among African Americans, because much of this behavior may be explained from the viewpoint of consciousness. However, it does appear that the three approaches mentioned above explain a considerable amount of human behavior and therefore should not be neglected in attempts to understand the experience of being Black.

Classical Conditioning Theory

The work of Pavlov became known to scientists outside of Russia when he was awarded the Nobel Prize in medicine in the year 1904 (Garrett, 1941). Originally, he had been investigating gastric secretions and noticed that certain stimuli caused these secretions spontaneously, very much like a reflex response. For example, when food was taken into the mouth of a dog (Pavlov worked almost exclusively with dogs), saliva flowed as a biological reflex, in response to the stimulation of the membranes of the mouth, lips, and tongue. He further noticed that under certain conditions the dog would salivate in response to stimuli other than the stimulation of the mouth with food. His interest in understanding the nature of these conditions led him away from the investigation of gastric secretions per se and focused him solely on the relevant conditions. It is important to understand that Pavlov's research in large measure was influenced by the philosophy of John Locke, who believed, contrary to Descartes, that all knowledge about the world and about ourselves comes from experience and reflection on experience; no one is *born* with any knowledge. Locke subsequently undertook the task of understanding how this knowledge was gained. He finally concluded that "Knowledge of the world around us began in sense perception and knowledge of ourselves in introspection" (*Encyclopaedia Britannica,* 1972, p. 191). He believed further that sense perception and introspection give us "ideas" rather than exact duplication of experience, and that knowledge is enhanced by the forming of connections between these ideas. Hence, Pavlov postulated that the automatic reflex of salivation, in response to food, could be made to appear also in response to a neutral stimulus *on condition* that a *connection* is formed between the food and the neutral stimulus. Instead of working with "ideas" and their interconnections, he investigated sensory stimuli, glandular (reflex) responses, and their interconnections. He used the term "conditioning" to refer to the establishment of the critical conditions, and the past tense "conditioned" implied that the conditions had been established. Placing a relatively hungry dog onto a table in a harness, Pavlov noticed that the dog would salivate at the *sight* of meat powder, without actually taking it into its mouth. He theorized that the dog had formed a connection between the sight of food and the tasting of food over such a long period of time (since birth) that the mere sight of food eventually evoked the same automatic response that originally was elicited only by taste. Hence, the *sight* of the food, since it caused unconditional salivation, was referred to as an *unconditioned stimulus* (US), and the response to this unconditioned stimulus was called an *unconditioned response* (UR). The unconditioned stimulus is referred to also as a reinforcer because it reinforces or strengthens the response. Pavlov also noticed that when he sounded a tone just prior to presenting the food, eventually (after 20 to 40 such pairings in the original experiments) the dog would respond by salivating to the tone alone, as illustrated by the following diagram:

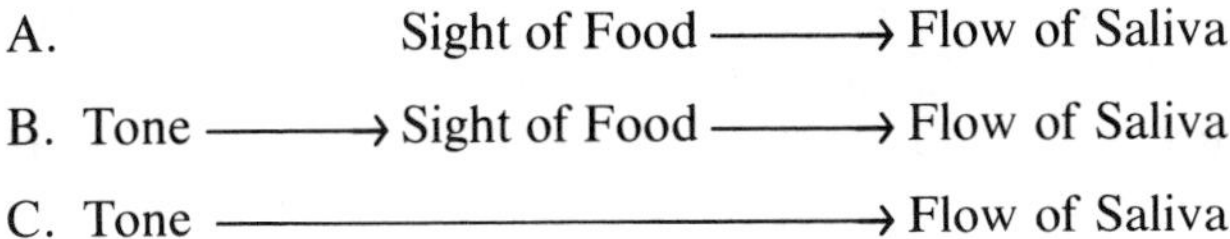

The tone was designated a conditioned stimulus (CS), since its effectiveness required special conditions, and the flow of saliva *in response to the tone alone* was called a *conditioned response* (CR). Thus, there were two stimuli (US and CS) and two responses (UR and CR), as a modification of the above diagram will illustrate:

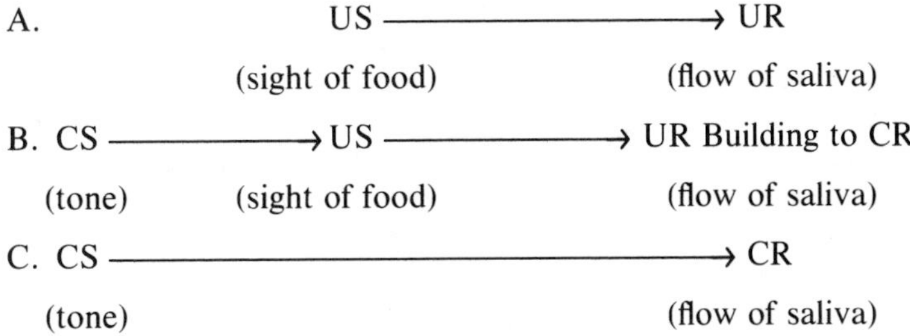

The reader might ask on what basis Pavlov determined that there were two responses, since the UR and the CR are the same. The answer is that by measuring the amount of salivation, he was able to demonstrate that the two responses were different quantitatively, though obviously the same qualitatively. In other words, there was more salivation in response to the US alone than there was in response to the CS alone.

A further observation was that as the CS was presented successively in the absence of US (step C of the diagram), the salivation became less and less until it eventually ceased altogether. At this point, Pavlov reasoned that the conditioned response had been extinguished or that *extinction* had occurred. Additional experimentation revealed that the tone (CS) prior to extinction, could be used in the place of the food (US) in order to condition the dog to a new CS, such as a flash of light.

$$\underset{\text{(flash of light)}}{CS^2} \longrightarrow \underset{\text{(tone)}}{CS^1} \longrightarrow \underset{\text{(saliva flow)}}{CR}$$

Eventually, the dog would salivate in response to the flash of light alone. It is possible to replace CS^1 with CS^2 and introduce a CS^3 (an entirely new stimulus) as the functional CS. Theoretically, this procedure of substitution, called *higher order conditioning,* could continue indefinitely, but extinction eventually would set in because of the absence of the true US. Another important concept discovered was that of *stimulus generalization.* This relates to the observation that the dog tended to respond with salivation to auditory stimuli that were similar to but not the same as the originally conditioned tone.

Additional research over the years has indicated that conditioning and extinction tend to be slow or fast depending upon the schedule of reinforcement. If the reinforcer is administered immediately and without fail after every presentation of the CS, the procedure is known as *continuous reinforcement;* if presented at varying durations after the CS or after varying presentations of the CS, it is called *variable reinforcement.* It has been found that continuous reinforcement results in rapid learning but also causes rapid extinction. Variable reinforcement, on the other hand, yields slower learning but results in slow extinction. It has been discovered also that the time interval between the CS and the US cannot be more than five minutes for conditioning to take place. These principles have been found to apply to a wide range of organisms and seem to explain much of human learning. In a famous experiment, Watson and Rayner (1920) applied these formulations to a fear response in a nine-month-old infant known as "Little Albert." Noticing that fear (UR) was caused by the presentation of a loud noise (US), the investigator presented a white rat (CS) prior to the loud noise a sufficient number of times for Albert to show fear in response to the rat alone. Prior to the conditioning, he had shown no fear whatever of the rat, although he had been exposed to it. Later, Albert showed the same fear in response to a white rabbit, a Santa Claus mask, and a cotton ball, thus illustrating the principle of stimulus generalization. One month later, he still showed fear of the same objects. Without an understanding of the conditioned relationship between the rat–loud noise association and the generalized rat–cotton ball relationship, Albert's fear of the cotton ball would be puzzling.

But most conditioning of humans does not take place consciously, and many responses on the part of residents in Black communities might be perplexing to those who are unaware of the subtle connections that take place between conditioned and unconditioned stimuli. The unique responses observed among people in inner-city neighborhoods, rather than being ancillary to the inhabitants themselves, are the logical, predictable consequences of this type of conditioning. A representative illustration is found in the relationship between Blacks and the police. The typical emotional reaction of Blacks to the police is either anger or fear (Breed, 1970) and probably represents a conditioned response. In order to specify the unconditioned stimulus in this situation, it is necessary to identify a factor (US) which automatically would cause the observed emotional response. Abuse would seem to qualify as such an unconditioned stimulus, and when occurring in connection with police (CS) would serve as the reinforcer. Thus, we have the following:

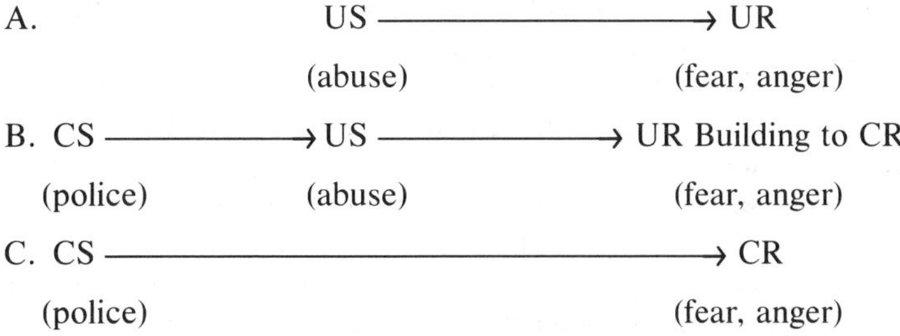

Just as in the case of "Little Albert," there might be generalization from police to similar stimuli, such as prison guards, firemen, and even non-uniformed people in various positions of authority. The fact that even Blacks who have not directly experienced abuse by police also show the same degree and frequency of fear or anger is explained by the work of Bandura and Walters (1963), whose research on modeling (also called observational learning and vicarious learning) has shown that observers of a reinforcement can be conditioned in the same direction as the overt participant. Because daily vicarious observations of police violence against Blacks may be made via television, the printed media, or word of mouth, there is an almost infinite capacity for vicarious reinforcement of the fear and anger throughout most Black communities.

The incidence and nature of police brutality towards Black males has been well documented (i.e., Dollard, 1937; Taft, 1950; Report of the National Advisory Commission on Civil Disorders, 1968; Asinof, 1970; Wolfgang & Cohen, 1970). Asinof points out that in the Black communities of America, the relationship between the citizens and the police is like that of an undeclared war; and that for a young Black man, confrontations with the police are the most predictable and the most brutal experiences of his existence. In explaining the customary nature of one such brutal event, Asinof reports that: "When police officers McCole and Repaci escorted the bleeding, handcuffed, stumbling figure of Larry Blutcher into the emergency ward of Cumberland Hospital, it was strictly a routine sight. There were no sickening gasps of horror, no indignant comments, barely a turning of heads" (p. 83). Since it apparently was viewed as just another dog-bites-man story, not a single newspaper in New York City carried the account, brutal though it was. Breed's study (1970), involving interviews with relatives, friends, fellow employees, and employers of completed suicides, showed that of the 42 Black suicides studied, 21 had had problems with the police and only 12 showed no police or other authority problems. Of those who had direct confrontation with police, four hung themselves while in jail, one committed suicide in a hospital after he was taken there by police, and four others died while being chased or sought by police (p. 18). Moreover, the interviews revealed abundantly spontaneous comments about the victim's fear of police. The interviewees, showing their own attitudes and feelings, expressed the belief that the victims, rather than having committed suicide, actually were killed by the police. In addition, it has been pointed out that in Black neighborhoods the police are viewed as "the symbol of white authority over community institutions" (Breed, 1970, p. 159). Breed also observed that the Black attitudes towards police extend to other authorities, thus demonstrating the pervasively generalized nature of these responses.

However, some of these negative feelings towards authority apparently result from nongeneralized vicarious experiences with authority figures, rather than representing generalized observational learning. In this regard, Wills-Barnett reports of a lynching mob led by the *Governor* of South Carolina, supplemented by his pledge to lead other such illegal actions "in order to protect the 'honah' of 'white womanhood'" (cited in Wesson, 1978). Wesson states further that because of incidents like this, the disrespect which Blacks show for the "law of the land" and its representatives is quite justified.

If there is the belief that Blacks of elevated prestige and status in the Black community are afforded more respect by the police, witness this personal account of humiliation and psychological emasculation reported by Dr. Alvin Poussaint (1970), the well-known Black psychiatrist and author:

> Once last year as I was leaving my office in Jackson, Miss., with my Negro secretary, a white policeman yelled, "Hey, boy! Come here!" Somewhat bothered, I retorted: "I'm no boy!" He then rushed at me, inflamed, and stood towering over me, snorting, "What d'ja say, boy?" Quickly he frisked me and demanded, "What's your name, boy?" Frightened, I replied, "Dr. Poussaint. I'm a physician." He angrily chuckled and hissed, "What's your first name, boy?" When I hesitated he assumed a threatening stance and clenched his fist. As my heart palpitated, I muttered in profound humiliation, "Alvin." . . .
>
> No amount of self-love could have salvaged my pride or preserved my integrity. In fact, the slightest show of self-respect or resistance might have cost me my life. For the moment my manhood had been ripped from me—and in the presence of a Negro woman for whom I, a "man", was supposed to be the "protector". In addition, this had occurred on a public street for all the local black people to witness, reminding them that no black was as good as any white man. All of us—doctor, lawyer, postman, field hand and shoeshine boy—had been psychologically "put in our place." . . .
>
> And if I, a physician in middle-class dress, was vulnerable to this treatment, imagine the brutality to which "ordinary" black people are subjected—not only in the South but also in the North, where the brutality is likely to be more psychological than physical. (Poussaint, 1970, pp. 16–17)

This reminder that the dominant culture tends to view Blacks as all being "in the same boat," regardless of differential accomplishments, was brought to our attention dramatically by the late Malcolm X (cited in Grier & Cobbs, 1970) who reportedly reminded a Black intellectual at a large university that the larger society refers to a Black scholar with a Ph.D. as "nigger." The observation is reinforced by current reactions to attempts towards affirmative action and equal opportunity in high status and high paying positions.

With the virtually ubiquitous capacity for observational learning in connection with police abuse, it is curious, from a scientific standpoint, that *any* residents of Black communities are able to avoid conditioned negative attitudes toward police. Significantly, Bandura and Walters (1963) have reported that vicarious learning is more likely to occur if the immediate learner and the observer are similar. Since most police brutality seems to be directed towards Black males rather than females, the males are likely to be more strongly conditioned through observational learning. These same researchers have pointed out also that the vicarious subject is more likely to learn the observed behavior of a prestigious rather than a non-prestigious model, thus underscoring the critically deleterious effects on the entire Black community when a Black man of the stature of Dr. Poussaint is ruthlessly vilified and degraded with absolute impunity.

Operant Conditioning Theory

The second major type of learning, operant conditioning, has been championed most notably by B. F. Skinner (1957). In this type of learning, the response, instead of being elicited from the organism as in classical conditioning, is emitted by the organism in a stimulus situation. When the desired behavior appears, it is rewarded and hence has an increased likelihood of appearing when the organism experiences the same or a similar stimulus situation a second time. If this second response is rewarded, there is an even greater probability of the same of a similar response on a third exposure, and so on. The rewarding of the response continues until it appears regularly in the absence of the reinforcer, in which case the response is said to be conditioned. The term "response generalization" is used to describe the observation that the conditioned response will appear in the presence of situations that are similar to but not the same as the situation of the originally conditioned response (Chaplin, 1975, p. 457). The continued withholding of the reinforcement, subsequent to the previously rewarded response, results in extinction. As in the case of classical conditioning, it is important to consider time factors in the presentation of the reinforcer. However, in operant conditioning it is critical to note that whatever behavior occurs just prior to the reward will be reinforced. Thus, the reward must be forthcoming immediately; otherwise some undesired behavior may be emitted and consequently reinforced. With this restriction considered, one should be aware that the same principles governing schedules of reinforcement mentioned for classical conditioning apply also to the operant model. In addition, the concept of observational learning (modeling) relates equally to operant conditioning.

Before considering examples of operant conditioning from the Black experience, the reader should be aware of several differences between classical and operant conditioning, besides the fact that the former applies primarily to elicited behavior while the latter tends to explain emitted behavior. First, in operant conditioning the reward serves as the reinforcer, while in classical conditioning the US is the reinforcer; second, operant conditioning, unlike classical conditioning, has no US; and third, in operant conditioning the reinforcer comes *after* the response, whereas in classical conditioning it comes *before* the response.

One can cite many examples of operant conditioning because of its applicability to more outwardly indicated behavior. In the early 1970s, this author was involved in the recruitment of "hard-core" unemployed Black men residing in a large metropolitan area. He soon learned that these out-of-work men had ceased seeking employment because their work-seeking behavior had been extinguished through a persistent lack of reinforcement. Most of these men told of rising daily, early in the morning, over a period of several months, in order to follow up want ads, complete and deposit employment applications, take civil service examinations, and so forth, all to no avail. That such job-seeking behavior becomes extinct through lack of reinforcement is no surprise to those who recognize the influence of operant conditioning principles. Those who are uninformed tend to fault the job seeker for not reacting in a way that would be both abnormal and unnatural. The reality is that it would be scientifically indefensible to expect a continuation of the job-seeking response in the absence of any reinforcement. What is amazing is that the searching response continued for as long as it did, in some cases for more than six months. Besides being suspiciously insensitive, attributing the extinction to predisposed laziness is yet another example of "blaming the victim."

Another example of operant conditioning was observed by this author when he was employed as a psychologist at a correctional institution for adolescents in New Jersey. While interviewing a Black youth who persistently was proclaiming his innocence of the charge for which he had been incarcerated, I asked why, if he were innocent, he had fled from the scene of the delinquent act. His reply: "Because the cops came." He then went on to explain that only a fool would remain at the scene and risk being sent to juvenile court where the rules of evidence, cross-examination, and due process do not apply.

The young inmate revealed several violations of which he was guilty but was not apprehended because he fled in time. As a function of observational learning, he recounted several instances of innocent people who had been incarcerated either because they were "too dumb to run" or were not swift enough. In his experience, "It's not whether you did it or not, it's whether they catch you or not." If continued freedom is the reward (as it probably is) and is contingent upon successfully running from the scene of a delinquent act, whereas remaining at the scene results in loss of freedom, guilty or not, then running away will be reinforced and remaining at the scene will become extinct. Another inmate, in response to the question "What is the thing to do if you see a train approaching a broken track?" (one of the questions found on the Wechsler Intelligence Scale for Children) replied, "Get the heck out of there because they might think you did it." The amount of direct and vicarious learning of this type that takes place in Black communities throughout the United States is virtually limitless.

We now can see that the behavior of Blacks towards police possibly is both classically and operantly conditioned. The fear or anger follows the classical model, while the *overt response* to the fear or anger (running away or showing some form of aggression) represents, if reinforced, the operant paradigm. Hence, the operant conditioning is superimposed on the circumstance of classical conditioning.

Grier and Cobbs (1968) explain the antiaggressive conditioning that has been directed toward Black males because of the threat that such aggression always has posed to the dominant society, which tends to respond with relentless retaliation. During slavery, the Black mother had to discourage her son's masculine assertiveness, because it would threaten the entire slave system and cause him to be killed. Today, aggressive Black masculinity still is viewed as a threat to the social system, and the Black mother unconsciously assists in the operant conditioning of her son towards the inhibition of aggression. This constant conditioning from slavery to the present, with its assorted rewards for nonaggressive behavior and punishment for aggressive behavior, apparently has had a debilitating effect on Black behavior in the form of response generalization. Hence many Black males tend never to express *any* emotion under *any* circumstances. This reaction will be discussed further in chapter 5.

The relatively recent focus of Blacks on Africentric standards, the previous attention to Eurocentric models, and the possibly threatening reversion to Eurocentricity, all might represent operantly conditioned behavior, particularly when the phenomenon of observational learning is considered. It is quite likely that the popularity of African hairstyles and standards of dress among many members of the Black community is related at least as much to social reinforcement as it is to pride in and identification with Africa.

Another view of operant conditioning has been presented by Seligman (1975), who has demonstrated the generalized effect of extinction. Using dogs, he administered 64 electric shocks from which the animals could not escape. At first, the dogs responded with a variety of movements, but since none of this behavior was rewarding, extinction eventually occurred. They simply did nothing and accepted the shocks passively. Later, the dogs were placed in an electrified box from which they could escape by jumping a barrier, but about 65 percent of them did not even attempt to escape, even though the shock was severe. By contrast, other dogs, not pretreated with the inescapable shock, also were exposed to the escapable shock, and 95 percent of them escaped by jumping the barrier. Seligman termed this extreme type of response-generalization "learned helplessness" and found that it explains a wide range of human behavior, including depression. The possible connection between this phenomenon and the responses of many Blacks to injustice and abuse (from which they cannot escape) should receive more attention than has been the case thus far.

Poussaint (1970) has observed that the lack of success in business enterprises among Blacks and the low achievement in school may be due to a learned inability to be normally aggressive, and his explanation seems to be very similar to the Seligman concept of learned helplessness. One promising note is that while 65 percent of Seligman's passively conditioned dogs did not leap over the barrier, 35 percent did escape, even though they had the same restricting experiences as did the others. Obviously, the negative experiences alone did not account for the helplessness response. The variable involved in the ability to cope with severely distressing stimuli from which there is no escape, and later to overcome the potential for generalized passivity, should be a major subject of research for Black psychology, because it seems to represent coping with hardship at the highest level. It may be that both consciousness and conditioning factors are involved in this process.

Social Learning Theory

The third major type of learning is represented by the social learning theory of Albert Bandura (1963). This theory, which also encompasses the observational learning discussed earlier, de-emphasizes the impor-

vards and punishments and focuses on the development ions regarding potential reinforcement. The social learning then, attempts to determine the manner in which individuals' periences cause them to anticipate various consequences for various behaviors. For example, John, an inner-city Black child or adolescent, might notice that a group of neighborhood youths verbalize disdain and utter invectives when they observe a police car approaching. Later, when with a group of his friends from the same neighborhood, he might curse and show displeasure upon seeing a police car nearby. John's reaction, according to social learning theory, is based on the expectation that his behavior will win the approval of his friends. In other words, the "social learning" is not a simple preservation and reenactment of the reinforced behavior that was observed in the initial group of neighborhood youths. Rather, it is a phenomenon in which the individual relates the present situation to past experiences and then decides on a course of action (Wortman & Loftus, 1988). However, social learning theory, because it regards both the external situation and the internal cognitions as being important in shaping behavior, does not negate the role of reward and punishment in shaping behavior. However, one must be aware that these cognitions, though logical, are not directly observable and therefore represent hypothetical constructs.

Conditioning and Language Development

In explaining and understanding the complexities of language development two major positions have been advanced: the nativistic view, holding that language is acquired by means of a natural process unrelated to learning, and the conditioning view, which sees language acquirement as being a consequence of conditioning. However, because "no child has ever mastered language without regular exposure to speech" (Wortman & Loftus, 1988, p. 24), reinforcement must play a part. Of the major learning theories, social learning theory seems to have the greatest likelihood of offering an acceptable explanation for this phenomenon. . . ." (Kennedy, 1971, p. 309).

Investigators tend to agree that language develops in various stages and that the initial vocal sounds made by infants are not learned but are based on physiological conditions, possibly stimulated by a language activator in the brain. That these early sounds are organic and are controlled by the maturation process is evidenced by work with deaf children, all of whom make these initial sounds. This earliest stage ends at approximately three months, when the babbling stage begins. During this second stage, lasting about three months, the infant's vocal behavior can be rewarded by social stimulation, and the significant adults tend to reinforce certain sounds while extinguishing others. Finally, during the imitation stage, which starts at about nine months, the infant becomes more susceptible to social reinforcement, imitating not only the sounds of others but also making self-made sounds. This susceptibility apparently facilitates the learning of language, since the infant is motivated by the reward of social approval.

Reportedly among the earliest to explain the infant's acquisition of language was John Locke. In his *Essay Concerning Human Understanding,* written in 1690, he "applied his explanatory principle of the association of ideas to the learning of language by children" (Garrett, 1941, p. 127). Locke's explanation of how the child learns the names of various objects, by having people show the object and immediately say the name until the child makes the connection and says the name in response to the object alone, is very similar to the classical conditioning theory of Pavlov. Also Allport (cited in Bandura & Walters, 1963) explained language acquisition specifically in terms of classical conditioning, but his explanation was criticized because it did not account for all of the observed facts. Although in their 1963 volume Bandura and Walters drew upon social learning theory to explain a wide range of behavior, including aggressiveness, sexual behavior, sex-typing, dependency, self-control, moral behavior, and deviant behavior, they did not bring the theory specifically and directly to bear on the learning of speech. Nevertheless, it might be reasonable to consider the likelihood that an infant learns language according to the principles of *both* classical *and* operant conditioning, with the operant learning superimposed on the classical paradigm.

Thus understanding language development would seem to require an investigation of the interplay of classically and operantly reinforced responses of the infant and child.

Language Development and Black English

It is possible that one major distinction between the adult Black speaker and the adult White speaker is that there tend to be differences, beginning with the critical stage of babbling, in the quality of not only the object-name associations, but also the socially imitated and socially reinforced responses. The interracial dissimilarity is due probably to the vast disparities in the environments of Blacks and Whites. Baratz (1971) reminds us that the myth of America as a "melting pot" seems to obscure the vast cultural differences between

Blacks and Whites and tends to confuse egalitarianism as a goal with equality as a fact. Reasoning from the myth, one insists on a perception of sameness between the races, rejects any suggestion of distinction, and reacts to any demonstrated differences as a sign of Black inferiority. Obviously proponents of the myth cannot acknowledge the existence of a discrete Black culture without experiencing stressful dissonance.

In explaining the origins of Black English, Smitherman (1977) tells us that when African slaves arrived on these shores, they at first developed a transitional pidgin in order to converse with each other (since they came from diverse language backgrounds) as well as with the White slavemaster and overseers. The pidgin became widespread and eventually developed into a Creole, which used English words while maintaining the basic structure of the West African languages. This English word–African structure has persisted until the present time. On this point, Smitherman says:

> Now, as anyone learning a foreign tongue knows, the vocabulary of the new language is fairly easy to master; to some extent, sounds are also. But syntactical structure and idiomatic rules require considerable time and practice to master. Moreover, the one item of language that remains relatively rigid and fixed over time is its structure. The formation of this Black American English Pidgin demonstrates, then, simply what any learner of a new language does . . . fit the words and sounds of the new language into the basic idiomatic mold and structure of the native tongue. (P. 6)

Later she indicates that Black English and White English differ most in grammatical structure, and that since grammar is the aspect of speech that is least likely to change over time, it is logical that Black grammar should be the last aspect of Black English to adopt the rules of standard English.

Although slave trading to America was abolished in 1808, slaves actually were brought from Africa as late as 1858. Hence, in terms of language usage, there were three classes of slaves: (1) recent arrivals who knew English; (2) those who were African born but had been in the United States for a longer period and were in the process of learning English; and (3) those, mostly born in the United States, who spoke good or exceptional English (Smitherman, 1977). Currently, among the islands along the Atlantic Coast of Georgia and South Carolina, we can find Black Americans (called Gullah or Geechee), who have retained much of their original African culture, language patterns, and vocabulary (Vansertima, 1976). In addition, Tu in Smitherman, 1977) found among these "sea islanders" African language structure but also the use of 6,000 West African words. Thus, as Smitherman informs us, Black language "looks back on an African linguistic tradition which was modified on American soil" (p. 15) and is defined as "Euro-American speech with an Afro-American meaning, nuance, tone and gesture" (p. 2).

Therefore, the language of Black people does not represent a compilation of erroneous usages; rather, it demonstrates adherence to the rules of a nonstandard dialect. In terms of phonology, morphology, grammatical structure, and so on, Black nonstandard English follows rigid rules just as do other dialects of English (Baratz, 1971; Dillard, 1972). The belief that it derives from thick lips, laziness, and/or other ethnic carelessness in pronunciation is borne of the sort of ignorance that serves to perpetuate the myth of Black inferiority in general. One must remember, however, that historically Blacks have communicated among themselves more in spoken than in written language. This is a function of an extensively documented oral tradition, involving storytelling, mythology, folklore, and the recording of historical events (Vasina, 1971). Thus, it is from the *spoken* language that one must evaluate the rules of Black English grammar, vocabulary, and overall word usage. A detailed examination of the grammar, vocabulary, and structure of Black English will not be attempted in this volume, especially since it has been done comprehensively elsewhere (Andrews & Owens, 1973; Dillard, 1972; Smitherman, 1977). However, a few of the more outstanding features should be noted. One such characteristic is the absence of the verb "to be." Andrews and Owens (1973) refer to this as subject-verb fusion, while Dillard (1972) and Baratz (1971) identify it as *zero copula,* or missing auxiliary. This structural form may be found with nouns ("He a doctor"), interrogatives ("How he find out?"), adjectives ("She weird"; "He crazy") and negatives ("We not leaving"). Other significant features, according to Andrews and Owens, are the double preposition ("I'd better get *on down* the road"), the on-for preposition ("What you waiting on," where "on" means "for"), and multiple (double and triple) negation ("I don't care if he don't never visit no more"). Dillard, in demonstrating the differential phonology of Black English, shows the Black speech variants of many standard English sounds involving consonant fusions. In one such combination, "th," he shows that Black English speakers pronounce it as "d" at the beginning of a word (initial "th"), as "v" when it occurs in the middle of a word (medial "th") and as "f" or "t" when it is at the end of a word (final "th").

Besides the pidgin and Creole aspects of the African's experience with English in the New World, there were additional modifications and distortions occasioned by the restrictions placed on the speech of slaves. Since slave masters and overseers held certain topics among slaves to be taboo, the slaves developed an undercover code, a "semi-clandestine vernacular" in order to confound the oppressor (Brown, cited in Andrews & Owens, 1973). Further elaboration of this point is furnished by Grier and Cobbs (1968) who report that among slaves:

> Language was used with a particular emphasis on double meanings. In fact, multiple meanings were imposed on language, as, for example, in the spirituals. To the uninformed listener the words spoke of religious longing; the singing provided a harmonious accompaniment to their work, and to the viewer all was piety and submission. The true meaning of the spirituals, however, involves a communication from one to another regarding plans for escape, hostile feelings toward the master, and a general expression of rebellious attitudes. As the language of any group provides a feeling of identity and group unity, the patois of the slaves came to take on a meaning and purpose for them. (P. 103)

Hence, the language of the Black speaker is part African, part English, and part furtiveness. Probably the most distinguishing aspect of this speech is the use of a rich and colorful vocabulary which "shows great spontaneity and creativity in the naming of experience" (Toldson and Pasteur, 1976, p. 111). Black vocabulary is resplendent with activity and force of utterance denoting feeling. This is demonstrated most cogently in a Western Electric community relations LP record (Winston, 1970), where two speakers engage in conversation using Black nonstandard English. Later, the same conversation is repeated in Standard English, and the two contrasting styles are evaluated. The verbal exchange points out not only the energetic, emotional expressiveness of the Black vocabulary and language style but also the differentially contextual usage of Standard English words. The dialog in the Black idiom uses such words as "clean," "mommy," "fox," etc., that have connotations and denotations to which most non-dialect speakers cannot relate. That one's "mommy" is not his mother or that one can be well-scrubbed but still not necessarily "clean" might be quite puzzling to the uninitiated. One can only guess at the confusion in cross-cultural communication that might result from the differential use of the few words mentioned above. When this disparity is multiplied by the unique usages of hundreds of other Standard English words, supplemented by a specifically distinct vocabulary, the capacity for intercultural misunderstanding becomes staggering.

This author vividly recalls an interview with a juvenile witness at a pretrial hearing in a youth center in Philadelphia:

Interviewer: "Did you see what happened?"
Witness: "Yeah."
Interviewer: "So what happened?"
Witness: "Well, see, it was like dis here. Me 'n ma man Toney, we was hangin' on the corner of ____________'n ________street. So, we was jis, you know, like, standin' 'ere rappin' when his o'lady eases up in this brand new short. Last time we seen her, she was pushin' a ol' raggedy deuce n' a quarter wit' no hubcaps. So he assed could he drive it, 'n she slid over, 'n he got in. Next thing I knew, da man he come ouda nowhere 'n assed Toney to show him some cards. So he looked at his o'lady 'n she went like dis here (witness shrugged). Den da man, he busted Toney."

Fortunately, the interviewer (this author), who was born and reared in the Philadelphia inner city, was able to translate the above description into Standard English for the Municipal Court judge. After the hearing, Toney's teacher, who had come as a character witness, asked and was told the meanings of "short" and "deuce and a quarter." After wondering how they could have come to have the meaning of "automobile," the teacher asked what could have motivated Toney's *mother* to steal a car! Imagine the degree of misunderstanding that must have taken place daily in that teacher's inner-city classroom.

Since Blacks and Whites live essentially in two different worlds, with differential reinforcement of object-name associations, we can see again the contiguous effect of both classical and operant conditioning in the learning of language. Suppose, for example, that the Black infant is being taught the object-name association to the stimulus "door." Since, in pronouncing Black English, one of the rules is to drop final "r" (Dillard, 1972, p. 309), the classical learning possibly takes place in the following manner:

US ——————→ UR
(parent says "do") (infant says "do")
(pronounced like "doe")

CS ⟶	US ⟶	UR building to CR
(parent shows a door)	(parent says "do")	(infant says "do")
CS ⟶		CR
(parent shows a door)		(infant says "do")

Through stimulus generalization, the infant will say "do" when shown a wide range of similar objects. Parents, of course, are careful to restrict the range of such generalizations, so that stimuli such as automobile hoods are not included. When the infant makes the classically conditioned response "do" to the relevant stimulus, the parent operantly reinforces the infant with praise, which further increases the likelihood that the response "do" will be made when the infant next sees a door. Whether the parent identifies the object as "door", "do," "tur" or "puerta" will depend upon the object-name associations to which the parent has been conditioned, and so on, down through the generations. Obviously, there is no legitimate basis for regarding associations made in one culture as being inferior or superior to those made in another. It is, of course, the vast expanse of differentially conditioned associations and responses that help to form cultural distinctions among humankind.

The point is that the Black speaker blooms in a cultural environment where there is reinforcement and imitation, often without awareness, of verbalized sounds that differ from those that are reinforced in White culture. This differential reinforcement, in addition to relating to language development, also accounts for the uniqueness of Black music, art, lifestyles, and so on. The scope of this Black-White cultural dissimilarity was underscored during the late 1960s and early 1970s, when large numbers of Black students began to gain admission to our nation's heretofore segregated public schools. The resulting "culture shock" and "culture clash" had a profound impact on both Black and White "melting pot" adherents. Often the most glaring symptom of the disparity was the use of language. Teachers and administrators at these institutions reacted on the basis of the same stereotypes and myths that are characteristic of less educated and less sophisticated members of society, and a wide range of programs began to emerge in the direction of eradicating the perceived verbal destitution. But as has been pointed out (Baratz, 1971), "It is precisely because Black nonstandard English is a well-formed language system that it cannot be eradicated. If you've spoken French, you don't necessarily forget it or change it when you learn English. The failure of thousands of English teachers to eradicate the 'language errors' of Black nonstandard English speakers is clear evidence that 'change' and eradication are not what acquisition of another dialect is all about" (p. 40).

Unquestionably, not all Blacks in the United States speak Black English, but "it is spoken by some ninety percent of the Black community — regardless of socio-economic status — including poets and professors, entertainers and elites, reverends and revolutionaries" (Smitherman, 1977). With utilization of this magnitude, its formal recognition as a distinct dialect is long overdue. It is not being suggested that Blacks should repudiate or subordinate Standard English, because it is required for successful interpersonal relationships in the United States, particularly in the vocational and educational arenas. What should be stressed is that in the process of teaching and learning Standard English, rejection or suppression of other languages is not required, as most immigrants to the United States are well aware.

CHAPTER FOUR

Perception and Consciousness

> There are . . . situations in American life in which the "Black Mind" sees it one way and the "White Mind" sees it another or does not see it at all. (Comer, 1972, p. 115)

There probably is no subject matter more fundamental to psychology than perception. In fact, the laboratory of Wundt, the founder of scientific psychology, was essentially a perceptual laboratory (Boring, 1929). Perception has been defined as "a group of sensations to which meaning is added from past experience" (Chaplin, 1975, p. 376).

Traditionally the subject has been discussed and explained in terms of how people organize the various sensory stimuli in order to develop conscious awareness of and give meaning to objects and events in their experiences. However, most research on perception, in addition to being restricted to vision and hearing, has been devoted to analyses of how we organize various shapes and sounds, with very little investigation of the more cognitive aspects. This is reasonable, since in order to know anything at all about the world, our senses must mediate. Otherwise our attitudes, beliefs, and other components of consciousness would be severely limited, if not absent altogether. In their chapter or perceptual organization, Goleman et al. point out that "without our senses, the world would not exist for us. . . . Your world would be silent, dark, void, without feeling, taste or smell. Your world is as your senses tell you it is" (1982, p. 159). From this latter statement, it follows that one's concept of the world, or any part thereof, is based on the translations that are provided by the senses, and consequently is not an exact replication of what is "out there"; and even this initial translation undergoes modification before the final perception is established. Thus, the likelihood of any perception being a precise duplication of reality is extremely remote.

This author is reminded of the following story told recently at a testimonial dinner:

Three professional umpires, who usually worked behind home plate, were asked to describe their major task. One said, "Some are balls and some are strikes, and I just call 'em as they are." The second said, "Some are balls and some are strikes, and I call 'em as I *see* 'em." The third said, "Some are balls and some are strikes, but they ain't *nothin'* till I call 'em." Though the remark of the second umpire would seem to summarize what we currently know about perception, the third umpire's statement may prove to be closer to the truth than we care to admit.

Understanding Perception

As an outgrowth of the many studies on visual and auditory perception, it has been found that the senses of the newly born are functional at the time of birth (Kimble & Garmezy, 1968) and that our perceptual habits are learned (Goleman et al., 1982). In an effort to understand this learning, a number of organizing principles that assist us in "making sense" out of our visual world have been identified. For example, after pointing out that no perception can give direct knowledge of the world and that our perceptual habits are learned, Goleman et al. (1982) demonstrate that our perceived world has a great deal of stability that is created through *perceptual constancies.* These constancies cause the basic features of an object to remain the same even though the physical stimulus changes. For example, an infant held close to one's face will project a much larger image on one's retina than will the same infant at a distance of 10 feet. Yet, one does not perceive the distant infant as being smaller or the close infant as being larger; the size remains constant. There are also constancies for shape, color, and brightness. Also, it has been determined that what we perceive is influenced by (1) nearness or proximity—stimuli that are close together are perceived as belonging together or of being part of the same pattern; (2) likeness or similarity—similar stimuli are perceived as belonging together; (3) inclusiveness—a pattern that utilizes all of the elements of a stimulus will be perceived more readily than one that uses only a portion of the elements; and (4) closure—we tend to fill in gaps in order to form a perceptual whole (Ruch, 1963).

Yet, merely explaining how we perceive various auditory, visual, olfactory, haptic, and tactual stimuli leaves a large void in our knowledge and understanding of how organisms experience their world.

Concepts, beliefs, attitudes, and other cognitive factors, being additional components of consciousness, should be studied as systematically as are the more customary aspects. Such an approach becomes even more important when we consider the aforementioned significance of consciousness in the lives of Africans.

Empirical information on the cognitive aspects of perception, though not completely absent, is unusually limited. Therefore, many of the formulations presented here must remain tentative, pending further research.

Our definition of perception implies that the initiator of any perception is the stimulus or stimulus situation that activates the consciousness of the organism through the sense organs. The organism then adds meaning to the stimulus, based on various "schemata" (Neisser, 1976) that are brought to the situation from past experience. We have many schemata stored in our minds, and each schema is constructed of expectations about the world and a readiness to respond in a particular way. Putting it somewhat differently, Ornstein (1977) explains that:

> As we mature, we attempt to make more and more consistent "sense" out of the mass of information arriving at our receptors. We develop stereotyped systems, or categories, for sorting input information.
>
> Simple categories may be "straight," or "red," or "loud." More complex ones may be "English," "interesting," or "in front of." In social situations, the categories may be stored as attributed personality traits. If we categorize a person as "aggressive," we might then consistently tend to sort all his or her actions in terms of this category.
>
> Our own previous experience . . . strengthens the category systems as it does a scientific paradigm. We expect cars to make a certain noise, traffic lights to be a certain color, food to smell a certain way, and certain people to say certain things. (P. 57)

In showing the unique and sometimes individually conflicting nature of perception, let's consider the following example: Each individual may have his or her unique scheme or category for "dog," which may be similar to the "dog" schema of others. When encountering a certain four-legged animal, the schema or category is activated. There are also schemata for "horse," "justice," "professor," "doctor," etc., ad infinitum. Since schemata derive from past experience, it is reasonable to expect that individuals with similar or dissimilar experiences would have similar or dissimilar schemata. The schemata also filter out unimportant information, so that stimuli not fitting the schemata will not be perceived. Imagine the confusion of the child and the adult when the child reports the presence of a dog standing in the street. The adult, upon inspection, perceives no dog. The child, still insisting on the presence of a dog, beckons the adult outside and energetically points to a *horse,* with the remark: "See the dog?" In this case, the child's schema for "dog" includes the adult's category for "horse." After an explanatory clarification from the adult, the child's categories for both of these animals would become similar to those of the adult, with the necessary exclusions and restrictions. Hence, there is an underscoring of the observation that schemata can be changed through new information.

Many of us have had the experience of "not seeing" something when it was "right before our eyes," or of not hearing something which was said loudly and clearly. Many famous and infamous impostors have been successfully deceitful by tailoring their behavior to various schemata so as to cause the desired perception. After all, how would one "know" that a person is a doctor, policeman, or meter reader, except that this person conforms to a certain schema? Often this author, while engaging in extension lecturing at the evening division of a local college, on the first day of class would sit in a chair near the center of the classroom, mingle with the students, and engage in typical classmate conversation. Then, at the scheduled time, he would walk to the front of the classroom, call the class to attention, and begin the lecture. Invariably, many students would assume him to be joking and suggest that he "stop fooling around before the professor comes in and catches you." Then there would develop a controversy as to his actual role, with most students lining up on one side of the debate or the other. Many students would remain skeptical throughout the lecture and others would voice concern about the stability of many of their other categories and schemata.

Scientific evidence of the role of differential experience in forming the various schemata has been shown by Greenfield and Bruner (1971) who, working with African youngsters, demonstrated that among the Wolof children who had never attended school, there is the assumption that their perception of a thing is the same as the thing itself. In a typical assessment of the Piaget concept of conservation, the child was given two tumblers, each half full of water, and reported that the tumblers had equal amounts of water. Then the youngster watched the experimenter pour the water from one of the tumblers into a tall, narrow container. The unschooled Wolof children tended to report the tall, narrow container as having more water than the remaining tumbler. When they were asked: "Why do you *say* the tall container has more water?", the children were silent, because the question apparently made no sense (recall the African's lack of distinction between belief and action, mentioned in chapter 2). However, when they were asked: "Why *does* the tall container have more water?" they responded quite easily but with explanations relating to magic. With only one exception, this type of explanation never had been found before by any investigator. Furthermore, the explanation of magic was not reported by any Wolof child who had been attending school for seven months or longer. Thus, there was the operation of an intercultural difference in perception, based on cultural factors unrelated to formal schooling, and an intracultural difference that was based on schooling. Greenfield and Bruner explained the perception of a magical influence in terms of the child-rearing practices that are characteristic of the Wolof family. These practices evaluate and interpret all physical acts and events in terms of social consequences. This subordination of the physical and focus on the social apparently causes the child to perceive a social explanation resembling magic: "You poured it and made it more." On the other hand, when the children poured the water into the tall container themselves, the physical and the social became distinct and they perceived the amount of water in the tall cylinder to be the same amount as in the tumbler, with the explanation that they were the same in the beginning. The observation that schooled Wolof children do not give the explanation of magic when they see the experimenter pour the water demonstrates the role of subsequent experience (in this case schooling) in the modification of perception. In another study of African children, Price-Williams (cited in Greenfield & Bruner, 1971) found that Tiv youngsters showed conservation at an earlier age than did the Wolof children, apparently because of differential experiences of a cultural nature. The Tiv culture, unlike the Wolof culture, encourages a manipulative approach to the physical world. Thus, the Tiv youngsters spontaneously played with the contents of the experiment's containers, whereas the Wolof youngsters never did so.

Another scientific example of the manner in which different schemata can cause differential perceptions was demonstrated by Hastorf and Cantril in 1954, when they gave questionnaires to Princeton and Dartmouth students subsequent to a game in which the star Princeton quarterback had been injured. Both groups of students perceived the game to be rough, and the Princeton subjects reported unnecessary violence directed towards their quarterback, while the Dartmouth subjects did not. Clearly, "the truth" in such a situation is relative, subjective, interpreted according to schemata, and therefore inaccessible in any absolute sense. Even scientists viewing the same data often come away with different perceptions of the facts, as Gould pointed out in 1981.

Perception and the Black Experience

The inability of Whites to share in the Black schemata was demonstrated by Myrdal's quotation of DuBois (cited in Clark, 1965):

> It is as though one, looking out from dark cave in a side of an impending mountain, sees the world passing and speaks to it; speaks courteously and persuasively, showing them how these entombed souls are hindered in their natural movement, expression, and development; and how their loosening from prison would be a matter not simply of courtesy, sympathy and help to them, but aid to all the world. . . . It gradually penetrates the minds of the prisoners that the people passing do not hear; that some thick sheet of invisible but horribly tangible plate glass is between them and the world. They get exicted; they talk louder; they gesticulate. Some of the passing world stop in curiosity; these gesticulations seem so pointless; they laugh and pass on. . . . Then the people within may become hysterical. They may scream and hurl themselves against the barriers, hardly realizing in their bewilderment that they are screaming in a vacuum unheard and that their antics may actually seem funny to those outside looking in. They may even, here and there, break through in blood and disfigurement and find themselves faced by a horrified, implacable, and quite overwhelming mob of people frightened for their own very existence. (Pp. ix–x)

Similarly, Mayor Richard Hatcher in his foreword to Comer's book (1972) asks:

> Does anyone understand that the jobless father often destroys himself, his family and his community? Does anyone understand the frustration of a mother who knows that her children will need the best education possible, but she can't afford it and the national community won't help pay for it? Does anyone understand that the young men who make city streets dangerous and destroy themselves with drugs could have been proud, productive citizens? Does anybody understand that these problems can destroy this country? (P. xv)

Another, perhaps more classic, example of the wide schism between Black and White perceptions is the conflict over why Black Americans have had and are having more difficulty than any other ethnic group in realizing "the American Dream." On this point, Comer (1972) points out that the disproportionately social, economic, physical, and psychological victimization of Blacks has been overlooked by Whites but has been seen in bold focus by Blacks. Giving substance to the Black perception, he reviews the increased concentration on high technology and its requirement for the level and type of education and training from which Blacks functionally have been excluded. The wretchedness of slavery, the breaking up of the Black family, the denial of land ownership to the poor and to most Blacks during a period when land grants and even land grabbing were proliferating, the cruel rejections and other hardships following emancipation, the poverty of Black education, the barring of Blacks from trade unions and professional organizations, and the persistence of anti-Black racism all stripped Blacks of a base on which to build a reliable means of meeting their basic needs. Blacks recognize these experiences as being vastly different from those of most immigrant groups and show little patience with those who cannot see the situation "like it is." In spite of the horrendous persecution of and injustices to Blacks in the United States, Comer (1972) tells us that:

> Much of white America does not see, feel or think that a wrong has been done and is still being done. It does not understand that compensation, justice and change are necessary. . . .
>
> In Homestead, Florida, after a black student protest, the South Dade High School voted 1,010 to 47 to keep the symbols of injustice that angered blacks: the nickname "Rebels," "Dixie" as the school song, the Confederate flag as the school emblem, Confederate uniforms for the band, blue and gray as the school colors, and the name "Rebel Review" for the student newspaper. Given American history like it is few things could be more insulting to black students.
>
> A white girl asked the leader of the black student group why he was angry. The black student told of his feeling. . . . "There I was, wearing the uniform of the man who fought to the death to keep my ancestors in slavery. That I looked ridiculous is not important. It actually hurt. (P. 113)

To most Blacks, it would seem to be unconscionable that anyone could not understand why a Black student would feel uncomfortable wearing a Confederate uniform while playing "Dixie" and carrying the Confederate flag. In like manner, there are conflicting Black-White perceptions of public welfare recipients, political figures, patriotism, capitalism, racism, religion, and sin (Comer, 1972). Understanding how these divergent schemata develop is the key to shedding light on the possible solutions to interracial and interethnic conflicts as well as other types of intergroup dissensions throughout the world.

Nevertheless, it is important to note that there are intra-group differences in perception among Blacks as well as inter-group differences between Blacks and Whites. Concerning this individually unique aspect of consciousness, it has been suggested that:

> Each person is an individual with a unique family history, training, profession, and unique personal interests. These background factors continously influence the differences in our personal consciousnesses. . . .
>
> Consider a scene in a park. . . . An artist walking through might note the quality of the light, the colors of the leaves on the trees, the geometric forms of the landscape. A psychologist might notice the people present, their mannerisms, interactions, speech patterns, A physician, looking at the same people, might notice not their interactions but their body structures and their health. . . .
>
> One man may be fascinated by a particular smell in the air, while another may be too immersed in his own thoughts and fantasies to register anything about the external environment. (Ornstein, 1977, p. 66)

An example of intra-group differences in perception among Blacks is the conflicting view of the United States Census. Prior to the 1970 Census, many civil rights organizations were urging full Black participation and cooperation in this national tabulation, especially because of the 1960 undercount. This undercount resulted in the loss, in the Black community, of $650 million in Federal money for vocational training alone, not to mention the loss in financial aid for public schools or forfeiture of additional legislators (Young, 1970). Blacks, then, should perceive participation in the census as being desirable and beneficial. To encourage participation, Blacks were reminded that: "The Census Bureau doesn't care about the information supplied by individuals. It can't use it in any way other than in compiling statistics. By law they can't give the information to the police, welfare, or housing authorities, or anyone else. In fact, once they feed the forms into the computer, you're just a number" (Young, 1970).

On the other hand, Walton (1970) tells us that the 1970 census campaign was a sinister plan for the further oppression of Black Americans. Quoting heavily from the Census Bureau's own documents, he showed that the 1970 census operation focused on Black males between the ages of 18 and 39 who were living in northern urban areas. This was in spite of the fact that the 1960 undercount was greatest in *southern* and *rural areas*. In contrast with Young's assertion that all census information is strictly confidential, Walton gives evidence that the census data is shared with 40 other Federal agencies. Trying to determine which of these two perceptions of the census is "true," and whether it is desirable or undesirable for Blacks to participate in the survey, gives us a perhaps disturbing view of the ambiguity and nonspecificity of reality as well as the inexactitude of perception. Blacks whose experiences and expectations are similar to those of Whitney Young will accept his perception, and the reverse will be true for those who side with Sid Walton. It is possible that many in the Black community will experience confused or ambivalent perceptions, resulting in much conflict when asked to participate in the 1990 Census.

Hence, perception is relative not only to racial/ethnic groups but also to persons *within* the groups. It also is relative to time. As an indication of this temporal relativity, the present author has found that Black students have developed a perceptual shift away from the Black pride, Black unity, and social protest concepts of the late 1960s and early 1970s (Houston, 1982). Administering the Black Consciousness Survey (Banks, 1970), to 96 Black female undergraduates in 1973 and 87 such students in 1979, he found that the mean Black Consciousness score was significantly lower in 1979 than in 1973 and that only 9 of the 40 items were answered uniformly over the six-year period. It was discovered further that 8 items were answered completely oppositionally in 1979, with the remaining items showing varying degrees of shifting away from the 1973 responses. For example, the 1979 data, in contrast with 1973, revealed *disagreement* with the views that a bank owned and operated by Blacks would be a good place to deposit one's savings and that the "natural" hair-style is dignified. Also, the 1979 sample showed *agreement* with the notions that: Blacks should avoid the race issue when conversing with Whites, America's racial problems should not be aired symbolically by Olympic athletes in an international forum, *individual* acceptance into American society should be a major goal of Blacks, and Blacks should "spread out" when in public in order to avoid voluntary segregation. Informal observations suggest that this temporal relativity embraces a wide range of additional perceptions relating to "Blackness," thus underscoring the relationship between the perceptual world and the passage of time.

CHAPTER FIVE

Black Intellectual Ability

> If one postulated sixteen grades of mental ability between Aristotle and the lowest idiot, the average Negro would be about two grades or one-eighth of the total distance below the average white. (Galton, cited in Tyler, 1965, pp. 299–300)

In discussing the matter of Black intelligence, it is important to recognize that the doctrine of biological determinism has been a strongly held belief among a wide range of scientists and philosophers from the time of the ancient Greeks (Gould, 1981). This doctrine holds that social and economic differences between and among classes, races, and sexes are due to heredity, and that society is simply an unfolding of this biology. Since various groups in society usually are placed in rank order, according to the presence or absence of whatever factors are under consideration, some groups are judged as being inferior and others as being superior. As far as race is concerned, the darker races usually are seen as being at the lowest ranked position. Among those who expressed a belief in the biological inferiority of Blacks were David Hume (the philosopher), Arnold Toynbee (the historian), Thomas Jefferson, and Abraham Lincoln, in addition to such leading scientists as Linnaeus (the great classifier), Georges Cuvier (the founder of paleontology and comparative anatomy), Charles Lydell (the founder of geology), Johann Friedrich Blumenbach (the founder of physical anthropology), and G. Stanley Hall (the father of adolescent psychology) (Gould, 1981; Tyler, 1965).

Since group differences, according to the determinists, reflect inborn distinctions, any differences among races, classes, or between the sexes logically may be construed as a reflection of heredity. However, this is a conclusion deduced from a deterministic premise and does not represent a scientific observation. Intelligence itself is a "reification" of a complex of human abilities which are condensed into a single number, assigned to each individual and then ranked in a series of purported worth, with oppressed groups at the bottom of the hierarchy (Gould, 1981). The primary basis for viewing intellectual ability as a unitary entity was the theoretical formulation of Carl Spearman (1904, 1927) who in his "two-factor theory" argued that the score one earns on a test of ability results from two factors: a specific factor, or "s," which varies according to the particular ability (e.g., shining shoes or balancing chemical equations) and a general factor, or "g," which is related to reasoning ability and may be strongly or weakly represented in a given "s." For example, an individual who is adept at balancing chemical equation would be endowed with high "s" for this activity but also would require high "g," since a high degree of reasoning would be involved. A skilled shoe shiner also would be high in "s" for his activity but would not need an enhanced level of "g" because little reasoning would be required. Spearman described "g" as a force or energy that was capable of being transferred from one mental operation to another. Though apparently enduring and unalterable within the individual, this "g" was thought to show interpersonal variability. Subsequent psychologists identified "g" as "intelligence" and "then all the intelligence testers had to do was to determine the level of 'g' through the medium of a few abilities known to depend on 'g' to a considerable extent" (Biesheuvel, 1943, p. 5).

History of Intelligence Testing

In terms of actually ranking racial groups according to a hierarchy of ability, the nineteenth century found craniometry to be the major criterion. This "science" was developed by the Philadelphia physician Samuel Morton, in an attempt to classify and rank the various races on the basis of skull capacity. According to Gould (1981), this was the first attempt to rank the races on the basis of numerically quantified, objectively obtained, comparative data. On the assumption that the skull cavity is an indication of brain size, Morton measured cranial capacity by filling the skull with lead shot and then pouring the shot into a graduated cylinder, so that the cranial value could be read in cubic centimeters. His results, on the basis of measuring over 1,000 skulls from both America and Egypt, showed that Whites had the highest cranial capacity and Blacks the lowest. However, Gould, in a 1977 correcting of errors in Morton's data, found no significant differences in cranial capacity among the races. "Yet, Morton was widely hailed as the objectivist of his age, the man who would rescue

American science from the mire of unsupported speculation" (Gould, 1981, p. 69).

Other investigators who gathered data purportedly indicating differences between the brains of Blacks and Whites were Robert Bean, a Virginia physician, and Paul Broca, a French physician. This is significant because brain size was assumed to be related to intellectual ability. In fact, Jensen (cited in Gould, 1981) claims that the correlation between I.Q. and brain size is .30, thus supporting the notion of I.Q. as a measure of innate intelligence.

What the measuring of heads was to the nineteenth century, the I.Q. is to the twentieth century, and the deterministic position seems to hold fast, as do the concepts of hierarchial ranking and the assignment of worth. The term I.Q., or intelligence quotient, was introduced initially by William Stern and was determined by dividing the individual's chronological age into the mental age and then multiplying by 100. The mental age was determined by means of a standardized test (EvEns & Waites, 1981). This sophisticated quantification was thought to be an objective measure of overall innate intellectual ability or intelligence, since the mental age was thought to be dependent upon inborn distinctions. Thus, intelligence became a hypothetical construct which was inferred from a test score. On this point, Chaplin (1975) says:

> In spite of the prevalence of intelligence testing, psychologists have found it difficult to define intelligence precisely . . . most of the psychologists who developed the early tests side-stepped the problem of the precise nature of what they were measuring and attempted to make their scales good predictors of scholastic achievement . . . most psychologists think of intelligence in much the same way that physicists think of time. Time is what chronometers measure. By the same logic, intelligence is what tests measure. (Pp. 263–264)

Thus, of the six definitions given by English and English (1958), the first explains intelligence to be "that hypothetical construct which is measured by a properly standardized intelligence test" (p. 268). One investigator (Joseph, 1977) identified seventeen definitions of intelligence, subdivided into those which were biological, educational, or faculty (emphasizing a faculty or capacity), while reminding us that "of all the terms in psychological literature, intelligence is probably one of the most nebulous" (p. 5). The present author, after reviewing numerous definitions, finds the one by Wechsler to be the most operational, in spite of his failure to relate it to the testing of Blacks and other minorities. Wechsler (1944) defined intelligence as "the aggregate or global capacity of the individual to act purposefully, to think rationally and to deal effectively with his environment" (p. 3). This definition seems to have the greatest applicability to Black people, because it takes into consideration environmental (cultural) factors, and seems to be related to the more enlightened approaches of Meeker, Mercer, and Feuerstein, to be discussed later.

The first standardized, individually administered intelligence test was the one developed in France by Alfred Binet in 1904 and published in 1905 (Joseph, 1977). This test first appeared in the United States in 1908, after Henry H. Goddard translated it into English for use at the Vineland Training School in New Jersey. The first actual revision and standardization of the scale for use in the United States was published by Lewis Terman of Stanford University in 1916. After revisions in 1937 and 1960, this test became the most widely used intelligence test in the United States (Samuda, 1975). However, Binet cautioned that the test was designed for classification and comparison, rather than measurement, and to assume that it compared anything either acquired or congenital was to exceed the scope of the scale (Joseph, 1977). Explaining further, Gould (1981) points out that Binet insisted on test users following three essential principles:

1. The scores are a practical device; they do not buttress any theory of intellect. They do not define anything innate or permanent. We may not designate what they measure as "intelligence" or any other reified entity.
2. The scale is a rough, empirical guide for identifying mildly retarded and learning-disabled children who need special help. It is not a device for ranking normal children.
3. Whatever the cause of difficulty in children identified for help, emphasis shall be placed upon improvement through special training. Low scores shall not be used to mark children as innately incapable. (P. 155)

However, all of these principles were ignored when his scale was brought across the ocean and translated into English for use in American schools. Thus:

> American psychologists perverted Binet's intention and invented the hereditarian theory of IQ. They reified Binet's scores, and took them as measures of an entity called intelligence. They assumed that intelligence was largely inherited,

> and developed a series of specious arguments confusing cultural differences with innate properties.
>
> They believed that inherited IQ scores marked people and groups for an inevitable station in life. And they assumed that average differences between groups were largely the products of heredity, despite manifest and profound variation in quality of life. (Gould, 1981, 157)

Similarly, Joseph (1977) tells us that "Goddard (in the United States) took only the slightest modified Binet scale . . . and stated that the test reflected innate capacity" (pp. 76–77).

Although the Binet scale was adapted for use with adults, it was designed originally for children, and in 1939 David Wechsler, who then was employed at Bellevue Hospital in New York, introduced an intelligence scale specifically for adults: the Wechsler Bellevue, Form I, for ages 16 and above. However, because this scale was constructed of items that had been validated by others, it continued to reflect school-related abilities (Joseph, 1977). Wechsler's 1939 scale was supplemented by the Wechsler Adult Intelligence Scale (WAIS), which was revised in 1981 (WAIS-R). He also originated, in 1949, the Wechsler Intelligence Scale for Children (WISC), for use with children and adolescents between the ages of 5 and 15. This scale was revised in 1974 (WISC-R). All of these Wechsler scales yield a Verbal I.Q., Performance I.Q., and Full Scale I.Q., and instead of requiring computation, these tests allow the determination of the I.Q. from a table, based on age norms. In addition to these widely used, individually administered tests, other psychologists have developed a wide range of group-administered, paper-and-pencil I.Q. tests.

Validity and Reliability

It is interesting to note the degree to which the admonitions of Wechsler, like the cautions of Binet, were ignored by the users of his tests. After acknowledging that economic status, social milieu, and "race" all "undoubtedly influence intelligence test results," and after admitting that limited knowledge precluded an evaluation of the exact degree to which these factors affect the test score, Wechsler (1944) states, "Thus, we have eliminated the 'colored' vs. 'white' factor by admitting at the outset that our norms cannot be used for the colored population of the United States. Though we have tested a large number of colored persons, our standardization is based upon white subjects only" (p. 107). Likewise, the 1949 WISC standardization sample contained no

Black children. Although the WAIS and its revision, as well as the WISC-R were validated with Blacks, the earlier tests often were and still are used invalidly with Black subjects. When this author was in his first year of graduate school he received supervised "training" in the administration and interpretation of the Wechsler Bellevue (Form I), using Black subjects. His Black supervisor advised him to "add 10 I.Q. points to the Full Scale score" in order to compensate for the fact that the test was invalid for Blacks. If this seems ludicrous, observe that many Blacks were classified intellectually, on the basis of this test, with no recognition of or consideration for the invalidity of the results.

Black-White Differences in Intelligence Testing

Based on a wide register of these individual and group tests, it has been determined that Blacks, as a group, tend to score approximately 15 points below Whites. The mean I.Q. score for Whites is 100, with one-half of the group scoring below 100 and one-half scoring above 100. Mathematical and statistical procedures, employing areas of the normal distribution curve, have revealed that for the general population an I.Q. of 100 lies at the 50th percentile. Thus, an I.Q. score of 115 has been found to be at the 84th percentile, meaning that such a score is greater than that earned by 84 percent of the standardization group. Similarly, an I.Q. of 85 is at the 16th percentile, an I.Q. of 70 lies at the 2nd percentile, and an I.Q. of 130 falls at the 98th percentile. Knowing the mean and the standard deviation of any normally distributed sample, one can determine the equivalent percentile point for any given I.Q. score, simply by referring to the relevant table within the appendix of a college-level textbook on statistics for the behavioral sciences.

Blacks, however, show a different distribution, with a mean of approximately 85 representing the 50th percentile for Blacks as a whole. It is this apparently racial difference in average I.Q. score, a finding acknowledged by both Black and White researchers, that forms the basis for the current controversy over basic causality. Hence, the conflict derives not from a dispute over the findings but from the differential *interpretations* of these findings. Shuey (1966) reviewed about 200 studies on Black-White I.Q. scores, covering all occupational levels and a wide range of ages. The forward to Shuey's book, written by Henry Garrett, articulates many of the negative assumptions regarding the basic determinant of racial differences in test score, thus fueling an ever-widening controversy. The difference of opinion is not whether but *why* racial differences in test score exist. In his forward to Shuey's book Garrett states that "the honest psychologist . . . should have no preconceived racial bias. . . . He is interested simply in uncovering differences in performance when such differences exist and inferring the origin of these differences" (Shuey, 1966, p. vii). Then, after suggesting that Blacks and Whites share a uniform environment, he goes on to state that the consistent Black-White difference in test score justifies the conclusion of a genetic basis for the disparity. Garrett's pronouncements about honesty and lack of preconceived bias italicize the tendency of the determinists, unlike the anti-determinists, to insist that they are completely objective in their search for truth and are rigorously impartial in stating the facts. As Gould states, "They portray themselves a purveyors of harsh truth and their opponents as sentimentalists, ideologues, and wishful thinkers" (p. 20). Among those in the past who have accused environmentalists of being politically motivated and socially idealistic were Cyril Burt, much of whose "data" later were found to have been faked, and Arthur Jensen (1969a) who stated, "Genetic factors in individual differences have usually been belittled, obscured or denigrated, probably for reasons of interest mainly on historical, political and ideological grounds which we need not go into here" (p. 28). Gould (1981) concludes that both hereditarians and environmentalists are influenced by political and other social factors. But since there seems to be a general tendency, especially in the United States, to accept biological explanations of human nature unquestioningly, and to reject the cultural causation position (unless there is compelling evidence to the contrary), he felt obligated "to demonstrate both the scientific weakness and the political contexts of determinists arguments" (p. 21). He then goes on to show a sinister array of faked data, modified photographs (to cause the desired appearance of mental deficiency), and altered pictorials, used by determinists to advance their claim. However, he also shows that many hereditarians, rather than consciously distorting their data, innocently fall victim to the self-fulfilling prophesy, which covertly guides them towards findings that are in keeping with their preconceived notions. Interestingly, Alfred Binet clearly recognized this possibility in his own research and took pains to guard against it (Gould, 1981).

The Heredity-Environment Controversy

Since virtually all researchers agree that both hereditary and environmental influences underlie behavior, the critical questions seem to be: (1) To what degree is intelligence inherited? and (2) Is the I.Q. score a measure of intelligence? The determinists reply "mostly" in response to the first question and "yes" to the second. The anti-determinists argue that the data do not supply evidence in support of the determinists' conclusions. As Kamin (1974) warns us:

> To assert that there is no genetic determination of I.Q. would be a strong, and scientifically meaningless, statement. We cannot prove the null hypothesis, nor should we be asked to do so. The question is whether there exist data of merit and validity that require us to reject the null hypothesis. There should be no mistake here. The burden of proof falls upon those who wish to assert the implausible proposition that the way in which a child answers questions devised by a mental tester is determined by an unseen genotype. That burden is not lessened by the repeated assertions of the testers over the past 70 years. Where the data are at best ambiguous, and where environment is clearly shown to have effect, the assumption of genetic determination of I.Q. variation in any degree is unwarranted. The prudent conclusion seems clear. There are no data sufficient for us to reject the hypothesis that differences in the way in which people answer the questions asked by testers are determined by their palpably different life experiences. (Pp. 175–176)

Whether we identify the problem as being between hereditarians and environmentalists, determinists and anti-determinists, or nature and nurture, it is essentially one of demonstrating or failing to demonstrate that the ability to earn I.Q. scores is passed genetically from parent to offspring. In this connection, it is germane to remember that Morton, Broca, and the other craniometrists were not concerned with cranial capacity, but rather with the "thing" called intelligence, which was assumed to be related to cranial capacity (Gould, 1981). And of course the lead shot was heralded as the scientifically operational definition of cranial capacity. Today, the lead shot and cranial capacity are replaced by the I.Q. test and the score derived therefrom. Apparently, the reification of intelligence via the size of the I.Q. score is superior to its reification through the number of buckshots.

One of the earliest attempts to use standardized, individually administered intelligence tests on large numbers of people from divergently different cultural, national, and ethnic groups was undertaken in 1912 by Henry Goddard, who was asked by the United States Public Health Service to evaluate the immigrants arriving at the Ellis Island receiving station in New York Harbor. As a result of the testing, it was determined that "83% of the Jews, 80% of the Hungarians, 79% of the Italians and 87% of the Russians were feebleminded" (Kamin, 1974, p. 16). This resulted in an increase of 350 percent in deported aliens for the year 1913 and 570 percent for the year 1914. That the Binet Scale, developed in France, standardized in the United States and administered by English-speaking psychologists, did not yield high scores when used to assess foreigners who were "just off of the boat" should not be surprising even to the unschooled. That professional psychologists, in the name of science, could relate the poor performance to "feeblemindedness" would seem to be virtually indefensible. As an example of test bias, on the Binet Scale, administered to these immigrants was the following question (Kamin, 1974): "My neighbor has been having queer visitors. First a doctor came to his house, then a lawyer, then a minister. What do you think happened there?" The correct answer was that someone had died: the doctor came because the person was sick; the lawyer came to make the will; and the minister's role was to preach the funeral (p. 176). All other perceptions, regardless of how ingenious or experientially relevant, were discounted.

But the Binet was not the only test used to assess the intellectual ability of immigrants. Mullan (1970), in a document originally published in 1917, reported on an apparently unstandardized test which he used in 1914 to establish normative data for the testing of immigrants at Ellis Island. The test was comprised of the following subtests: (1) arithmetic; (2) non-arithmetic memory; (3) a "transitional test" involving the reciting of the days of the week forward and backward, recognition of opposites, naming of animals, naming of colors, the perception of weights, and the translation of coins into larger and smaller denominations; and (4) non-arithmetical reasoning. Although the tests were administered to immigrants from 21 separate countries, Mullan admitted that his only translator was "an interpreter who spoke Italian, Spanish, and German" (p. 5). That the language barrier probably was an uncontrolled variable serving deleteriously throughout the testing is suggested by the following account of the arithmetic testing of one subject:

> When asked how much are 3 and 4, a bright Norwegian responded 12. He was then asked how many are 3 apples and 4 apples, to which he replied 12. He succeeded in getting all the other additions tests, even getting 17 + 13 + 9 + 4 with ease. In the first trial he evidently assumed that 3 × 4 was wanted and held on to this faulty assumption in

> the second trial. Mistakes are often caused by similar false assumptions on the part of the normal subject . (P. 21)

Another uncontrolled variable, possibly motivation, is indicated by the observation that:

> A number who failed at trial 2 succeeded at a third trial, but the result of such trial was not officially recorded.
>
> Sometimes, after a subject has been doing well, he suddenly begins to do poorly. Some peculiar motive has influenced his action. In some of these cases it is believed that the immigrant feels that he is in for a long examination and wishes to terminate it by slipshod answers. (P. 21)

On one of the memory tests, in which the subject was required to repeat a short story about a man and a pig, a Spanish immigrant was given a zero (out of a possible score of 20) when he replied, "I don't understand. You are saying something about a Christian and an animal on earth" (p. 37). Of Mullan's 16 examples of responses to this item, 4 were from Spanish immigrants, and all 4 examinees were given a score of zero out of a maximum score of 20. Mullan's volume is replete with examples of cross-cultural confusion, culturally diverse perceptions, and miscommunications, all pointing to the questionable validity of his results. Even ostensibly nonverbal subtests revealed cultural biases that operated against the examinees.

With the advent of World War I and the need to assess the intelligence of large numbers of draftees, it would have been unthinkable to attempt *individual* assessment, as was required by the Binet Scale and the test developed by Mullan. Under the direction of Robert Yerkes, then president of the American Psychological Association, United States Army psychologists developed two *group* tests which eventually were administered to 2 million men (Kamin, 1974). One test was the "Alpha," for use with literate draftees; the other was the "Beta," for those who were illiterate. After the war, according to Kamin, statistical analyses were conducted on the scores of 125,000 of the men, including 12,407 draftees who were born in foreign countries. These analyses showed that of the foreign-born draftees, the ones who scored the highest were born in England, Holland, Denmark, Scotland, Germany, and Sweden. Those who scored lowest were born in Russia, Poland, Italy, Greece, and Turkey. The highest scores of all foreigners were obtained by immigrants from England! These "scientific facts" were brought to the attention of the United States Congress, which already had been advised of the results of the testing at Ellis Island. In fact, as a consequence of the Ellis Island results, Kamin reports that the printed media of the period contained many articles that reflected a public uproar over the lack of "quality control" regarding the immigrants. To believe that the mental testers were not then (and are not now) aware of the political connotations and overtones of their "results" is difficult to accept. This renders even more curious the hereditarian's persistent assertion that it is the *environmentalist* who is driven by political and idealistic motives.

There is the strong suggestion that all of these tests were used to screen thousands of immigrants and that the results were seized upon by those who were influential in having Congress legislate this country's first mandated national quotas on immigration. The initial restriction was in the form of a 1921 amendment to the existing immigration law of 1875. The more circumscriptive legislation was the Johnson-Lodge Immigration Act of 1924, which reduced the quotas of each foreign country from the 1921 proportion of 3 percent to a new quota of 2 percent, based on the census of 1890 (Kamin, 1974). As Kamin points out, the purpose of using the earlier census as a base was to militate in favor of the Northern Europeans and against those from southeastern Europe (the "Mediterraneans"), since the latter scored lowest on the I.Q. tests, and since these "inferiors" did not begin arriving until after 1890. Prior to the enactment of the Johnson-Lodge Immigration Act, the results of the Ellis Island testing and the U.S. Army sampling had been entered as indirect testimony into the proceedings of various congressional subcommittees on immigration, expressing the view of I.Q. heritability and showing confidence in the assessment methods developed by psychologists. One "expert" actually stated, in a document included in the appendix to the January 1923 hearings of the House Committee on Immigration and Naturalization, that based on I.Q. test scores, there should be serious objection to immigration from Russia, Poland, Greece, and Turkey. In a 1924 hearing, this committee was told that if mental tests had been available prior to 1890, more than 6 million foreigners then living in the United States never would have been admitted and that millions of people had been admitted whose intelligence was closer to that of the average Black than to that of the average American White (Kamin, 1974). Here, in addition to the problem of *future* immigrants, we see the germination of a concern about the "inferiors" already present in the American population, thereby further placing the present-day debate over Black-White intellectual differences into historical perspective. The Ellis Island and U.S. Army testing results not only provided the "scientific" data that was needed to exclude certain foreigners who were perceived to be generally inferior but also stimulated speculative accounts from others of influence. A published article written by Professor Nathaniel Hirsch of Harvard in 1926, for example, stated: "I have seen gatherings of the foreign born in which narrow and sloping foreheads were the rule. . . . In every face there was something wrong—lips thick, mouth coarse . . . chin poorly formed . . . sugar loaf heads . . . goose-bill noses . . . a set of skew-molds discarded by the creator. . . ." (Kamin, 1974, p. 28).

In addition to analyzing the Army test scores of the 12,407 foreign born draftees, researchers also evaluated the scores of 25,575 American Blacks and compared them with those of 55,838 American Whites. The results showed, as expected, that the mean scores of the Whites, on both the Alpha and the Beta, surpassed those of the Blacks. In view of the strongly held and widely promulgated belief, supported by psychologists and "verified" by the results of the testing of immigrants, that I.Q. scores represented inborn ability, the data seemed to provide empirical evidence of Black intellectual inferiority. However, a closer examination of the data revealed that Blacks from the North earned higher scores that did Blacks from the South, northern Whites surpassed southern Whites and, most interestingly, *northern Blacks outscored southern Whites* (Montagu, 1963; Tyler, 1965). But when geographical locations was controlled, the difference favored the Whites, both North and South, with two exceptions: Blacks from Kentucky earned a mean Beta score that was higher than the mean for Whites from the same state, and a similar discrepancy in favor of Blacks was found for draftees from Ohio. In fact, the Beta scores of the Ohio Blacks were higher than those of Whites from 27 states, 13 northern and 14 southern (Montagu, 1963). In summarizing the results of these data, Montagu states:

> Thus, the lowest scores made on any test by Negroes and whites are invariable to be found in the South—the deeper the South the lower the score. The depressed socio-economic state of the South as compared with the greater part of the rest of the United States is an unfortunate fact. It is, therefore, not surprising that both Negroes and whites in the South should do worse on the tests than their fellows in any other part of the Union; and, since conditions are invariably worse for Negroes than for whites, that the Negroes should do worse than the whites.
>
> In short, these findings show that, whatever inherent differences may exist between Negroes and whites, intelligence, or whatever it is that was measured by these tests, is to an

> appreciable extent determined by external factors, and that, when these external factors are favorable to one group and unfavorable to another, the favored group will excel the unfavored one. The superior achievement of the Negroes from some states as compared with the whites from others cannot be explained on any other grounds. From whatever position the matter is viewed, this is the only possible explanation. (P. 111)

But there developed not just another explanation but two other explanations, one of which was a specification of Montagu's "external factors." The weaker argument, developed by the determinists, whose position obviously was threatened by the re-examined Alpha and Beta results, became known as the *selective migration hypothesis* (Tyler, 1965). This position argued that the most able, intelligent, and ambitious of the blacks abandoned the South to seek enhanced opportunities and generally greater freedom in the North. The result was a positively skewed Black I.Q. distribution in the South and a disproportionate representation of higher I.Q. Blacks in the North. The Army test results, according to this theory, represented nothing more than empirical evidence of this skewing. The major limitation of this hypothesis was that it did not explain the superior scores of the northern *Whites* as compared with southern *Whites.*

The second explanation of the superiority of northern Blacks over southern Whites was the *educational opportunity hypothesis,* which held that the differences were due to the greater educational opportunities available in the North. This explanation would seem to apply also to the discrepancy between northern and southern *Whites.*

In a series of studies designed to test the two hypotheses, Otto Klineberg (cited in Tyler, 1965) found that: (1) there were no significant differences between the academic grades of children who left the South and those who remained, and (2) Stanford Binet I.Q.s of southern-born children living in New York City were positively correlated with length of residence in New York. In a more rigidly scientific study involving over 1,500 Black children in the Philadelphia public schools, E. S. Lee found results very similar to those of Klineberg (cited in Tyler, 1965). In addition to the native southern children, Lee's study included 636 Philadelphia-born children, 212 of whom had attended kindergarten and 424 of whom had not. They were tested with the Philadelphia Test of Mental and Verbal Ability, in grades 1A, 2B, 4B, 6B, and 9A. The results showed that at each grade level, those who had been exposed to the kindergarten experience were superior in I.Q. score to those who had not attended kindergarten, thus suggesting the positive effect of kindergarten experience on I.Q. score. However, it is possible that the kindergarten attendees were higher in I.Q. score initially; unfortunately, there was no indication of what Lee had controlled for this factor.

This educational opportunity–selective migration dispute has evolved into a rather profound controversy over the relative roles of nature (heredity) and nurture (environment) in the development of the I.Q. The argument seems to ebb and flow, resurfacing with sociopolitical issues. While the immigration issue was the related focus of the first few decades of this century, the matter of school integration apparently was the stimulus for the rekindling of the dispute in the 1950s. In 1954, the United States Supreme Court, in the landmark case of *Oliver Brown et al. vs. Board of Education of Topeka,* ruled that separate educational facilities are unequal and therefore violate the Fourteenth Amendment. This decision and mandate again raised the age-old polemic about Black intelligence and educability. Significantly, in 1956, Dr. Frank C. J. McGurk, then Associate Professor of Psychology at Villanova University, stated in a weekly news magazine:

> If we in America are going to make any sense out of the Supreme Court's desegregation decision, we will have to be more factual about race differences, and much less emotional. We can have our dreams, if we like to dream, but we should be willing to distinguish between dream and reality. Already, we have gone too far toward confusing these two things.
>
> As far as psychological differences between Negroes and whites are concerned, we have wished—and dreamed—that there were no such differences. We have identified this wish with reality, and on it we have established a race-relations policy that was so clearly a failure that we had to appeal to distorting propaganda for its support. When that, too, failed, we appealed to the legal machinery to do what nature was not content to do. (P. 92)

After reviewing the World War I U.S. Army test data and several other studies purporting to "prove" that Blacks are inferior to Whites in intelligence, McGurk asserts that:

> Regardless of our emotional attachment to the school desegregation problem, certain facts must be faced. First, as far as psychological-test performance is a measure of capacity for education, Negroes as a group do not possess as much

> of it as whites as a group. This has been demonstrated over and over. (P. 96)

Then, after presenting only those studies that supported his bias, he states:

> Lastly, it should be remembered that the studies described in this article are not a selection of studies intended to emphasize a point of view. They are the only existing studies that relate to the problem. That there is need for more information about this problem is more than clear, but with our emotions what they are, it is becoming less and less likely that anything better than speculations and distortions will appear. (P. 96)

In a later issue of the same news magazine, 18 nationally and internationally renown social scientists presented a rebuttal to the McGurk article, citing, among other evidence, the following 1950 statement by a group of social scientists meeting in UNESCO House in Paris:

> Whatever classification the anthropologist makes of man, he never includes mental characteristics as part of those classifications. It is now generally recognized that intelligence tests do not in themselves enable us to differentiate safely between what is due to innate capacity and what is the result of environmental influences, training and education.
>
> Wherever it has been possible to make allowances for differences in environmental opportunities, the tests have shown essential similarity in mental characters among all human groups. In short, given similar degrees of cultural opportunity to realize their potentialities, the average achievement of the members of each ethnic group is about the same. Does race really make a difference? (1956, p. 74)

After presenting similar statements by two additional groups of scientists, based on extensive research, the authors inform us that:

> These statements still stand, and in our judgment represent the consensus among experts who have studied this question as objectively and as scientifically as is at present possible. We know of no new research which would reverse these conclusions. (P. 74)

With this, one would think that the matter should have been laid to rest. Yet, in 1969, when Head Start and other compensatory programs were being assessed, Jensen's article appeared, with the suggestion that compensatory education has failed mostly because the Black child "has a lower genetic potential to benefit from any compensatory help given" (Pyle, 1979, p. 52). In addition to having been renounced by individual dissenters, Jensen's position has been rejected by the American Association for the Advancement of Science (O'Toole, 1976). Yet, the argument continues and probably will reduce to a simmer only to be reactuated in response to some future sociopolitical issue.

Let us now take a closer look at the problem from the viewpoints of both the hereditarians and the environmentalists.

The Case for Hereditarians

The conviction that I.Q. score is a measure of innate intelligence is an inference based on two assumptions: (1) that there is an underlying "thing" related to I.Q. in a one-to-one way, and (2) that this "thing" is normally distributed in a correctly chosen reference population (Layzer, 1976). Although it is difficult, at best, to demonstrate the reality of something that cannot be observed directly, it is less arduous to infer its existence on logical grounds. Since all behavior seems to be an emergent end-product of the interaction between heredity and environment, controlling one of these variables tends to produce results logically attributable to the other. If, for two people or two groups of people, environmental factors are held constant, then any observed differences in behavior could be related to hereditary influences. With heredity held constant, any differences may be ascribed to environmental factors. But, as Tyler (1965) reminds us:

> Historical and economic factors have produced a social structure in which persons of different races are exposed to quite different environmental influences throughout their lives. If anatomical proportions are not entirely determined by heredity, most psychologists agree that mental abilities and personality traits are even less so. Consequently, before we can answer the question as to whether there are fundamental biologically-determined mental differences between races, we must either make the proper allowance for the effects of unequal education and socio-economic status, or we must find groups of subjects of the races to be compared who have not been exposed to these inequalities but who still are representative of their respective populations. In order to do the first of these things, we need to know a great deal more than we do now about the specific effects of all sorts of environmental influences on mental development, the subtle factors such as the emotional responsiveness and the goals and values of the family,

> as well as the obvious factors such as material standard of living and amount and quality of education. To do the second is practically impossible. We cannot find, in this country, sizable groups of whites and Negroes for whom environmental influences have been equal in any scientifically adequate sense of that term. (P. 303)

Because of this limitation, scientists have begun to focus on the study of monozygotic twins, since the *heredity* of such pairs ostensibly is uniform. Hence, any differences in the I.Q. scores of identical twins may be attributed logically to environmental effects; the more dissimilar the environments, the greater would be the expected I.Q. disparity. Monozygotic (identical) twins, often referred to in the scientific literature as MZ twins, result when one sperm fertilizes an ovum and two individuals are produced. When two different sperms simultaneously fertilize two separate ova, fraternal twins will result. This latter type is known as dizygotic (DZ). Since MZ twins come from the same ovum, they are believed to have identical genes, whereas DZ twins have no greater genetic similarity than do ordinary siblings. Therefore, a pair of MZ twins gives us the only opportunity to study two persons who have the same genetic composition (Kamin, 1974; Tyler, 1965). Although MZ twins and other kinships have not been separated deliberately for research purposes, many have been reared apart from birth because of various situational circumstances and have been tested for I.Q. score.

The Concept of Correlation

In view of the use of correlation coefficients in the results and discussions of virtually all studies dealing with the heritability of the I.Q., using twins and other family members, it is important that the reader have some knowledge of the notion of correlation. Correlation is essentially a co-relationship: the degree to which changes in one variable are accompanied by changes in another. For example, using a fairly large sample of students, one might compare scores on the Verbal section of the Scholastic Aptitude Test (SAT) with final examination grades in freshman English. If the students who earned high SAT scores also tended to earn high grades on the English final exam, and the low scorers on the SAT were also low scorers on the English exam, there would be a *positive* correlation. If on the other hand the students who earned high SAT scores tended to have *low* grades on the English exam and vice versa, there would be a *negative* correlation. If there were no relationship between the SAT scores and the exam grades, the correlation would be zero. It is possible also to evaluate the relationships among several variables simultaneously, such as the relationship between college grade-point average and the combination of SAT-Math, SAT-Verbal, and high school rank; but this type of correlation should not concern us here.

The strength of the association between any two variables can be measured mathematically and expressed in a single number called the correlation coefficient. This coefficient ranges in value from +1.00 (perfect positive correlation) to −1.00 (perfect negative correlation), with all gradations in between. The sign of the correlation tells us the direction of the relationship. "The absolute magnitude or size of the coefficient—that is, ignoring the plus or minus sign—indicates the strength of the relationship between the two variables. A correlation of +0.95 reflects a very strong relationship between X and Y. A correlation of −0.95 also reflects a very strong relationship" (Shavelson, 1981). The procedures involved in the actual computation of this coefficient will not be reviewed here, but the reader is encouraged to explore this matter through course work in psychological or educational statistics.

In investigating the I.Q. scores of MZ twins, the researcher locates a sample of twins who have been reared in separate homes since birth, administers an I.Q. test to all subjects, and then computes a correlation coefficient to determine to what degree, if any, the I.Q. scores of the pairs are related. Because heredity is presumed to be uniform for each pair, a highly positive correlation among the I.Q.s of acceptable numbers of MZ twins reared in contrasting environments would suggest the superiority of hereditary influences over environmental factors. The reverse would be true for a positively low correlation, while a negative correlation would be most unexpected.

Jensen's 1969 report refers to three statistically analyzed studies of MZ twins reared apart, involving a total of 116 pairs. In a 1937 study of 19 pairs by Newman, Freeman, and Holzinger, the correlation was .77; in a second study of 44 pairs by Shields in 1962 it was also .77; and in the third study the correlation was .86. However, this latter study was conducted by Cyril Burt, whose work has been discredited since the publication of Jensen's document. In addition to the three studies mentioned by Jensen, Kamin (1974) cites a fourth study by Juel-Nielsen, which yielded a correlation of .62. Interestingly, Kamin reported the 1937 study by Newman et al. as showing a correlation of .67 as opposed to Jensen's citation of .77. Kamin's careful evaluation of all of these studies reveals that, based on a wide range of questionable or imprecise methodological considerations relating to procedure, materials, and experimental design, all of the correlations probably were inflated. One inflating factor, which seemed to confound two of the three seriously considered studies, was that of age-I.Q. intermingling. Virtually all I.Q. tests have been tried out on sample populations (standardized) in such a way as to produce an average I.Q. of 100, regardless of the age of the examinee. This means that the *average* I.Q. should be 100 for 10-year-olds, 12-year-olds, 16-year-olds, 20-year-olds, and so on. However, if during the standardization of the test, items at one age level were overly difficult, while those at another age level were overly easy, then individuals would show varying I.Q.s depending on their age at the time of testing. This would mean that I.Q.s of twins, since they are exactly the same age, would fluctuate together. The result would be that if several pairs of twins, varying in age, are tested at a given point in time, the correlation in I.Q. might be due in large measure to a defect in the age standardization of the test (Kamin, 1974).

It is of interest that in the Shields study, the MZ pairs of separated twins reared in non-related families showed I.Q. correlations of .47, while for those living in separate but highly similar environments, the correlation was .99. These results seem to suggest a strong environmental influence and causes one to wonder what the correlation would be for MZ twins reared in *extremely* dissimilar environments.

In attempting to evaluate I.Q. correlations among kinships other than MZ twins, the task is quite complicated because of the intermingling of heredity and environment. As Kamin points out:

> The demonstration that kinfolk resemble one another . . . cannot in itself establish that the trait is genetically determined. The difficulty is that relatives share more than common genes. They also share a basically similar familial environment. . . . This obvious confounding of genetic and environmental factors poses fundamental difficulties for the interpretation of kinship correlations in I.Q. (1974, p. 74)

The most thorough summary of familial data regarding the I.Q. was provided by Erlenmeyer-Kimling and Jarvik (cited in Kamin, 1974). These data indicate that studies conducted by others have compared dizygotic twins (DZ), non-twin siblings, unrelated persons, cousins, parents versus offspring, grandparents versus grandchildren, and uncles or aunts versus nephews and nieces. Jensen reviewed studies like these, in addition to research on MZ twins, and concluded that heredity accounts for about 80 percent of the variance in I.Q., leaving only 20 percent for environmental influences. In addition, Jencks (cited in Layzer, 1976), who has made "the most elaborate hereditability analysis of the I.Q. data" (p. 223), suggests that heredity accounts for 25 percent to 65 percent of I.Q. variance, depending on the level of probability. On the other hand, Kamin's determination from essentially the same data used by Jensen and Jencks was that there was "no evidence sufficient to reject the hypothesis of zero I.Q. hereditability. The availability data are at many critical points almost wholly unreliable" (pp. 104–105). Even when he reviews the studies of adoptive children, who have different genes but ostensibly the same environment, Kamin finds no support for the notion that I.Q. is inherited to any degree. Although Jensen continues to defend his position with a variety of arguments (e.g., Jensen, 1969b, 1980), the hereditarians have not been successful in showing a scientific basis for rejecting the hypothesis that there are no innately intellectual differences between and among any of the races of mankind.

But if the conflict were to be resolved in favor of the hereditarian position, with a consensus that I.Q. differences among *individuals* is due mostly to heredity, it still would not follow that intellectual differences between and among *races* are also due to heredity. As Jensen (1969a) readily admits:

> All the major heritability studies reported in the literature are based on samples of white European and North American populations, and our knowledge of the heritability of intelligence in different racial and cultural groups within these populations is nil. For example, no adequate heritability studies have been based on samples of the Negro population of the United States. (Pp. 64–65)

Giving indisputable evidence that his belief in the genetically inferior intelligence of Blacks derives from an untested hypothesis with no direct evidence, Jensen states that:

> There is an increasing realization among students of the psychology of the disadvantaged that the discrepancy in their average performance cannot be completely or directly attributed to discrimination or inequalities in education. It seems not unreasonable, in view of the fact that intelligence variation has a large genetic component, to hypothesize that genetic factors may play a part in this picture. . . . The fact that a reasonable hypothesis has not been rigorously proved does not mean that it should be summarily dismissed. It only means that we need more appropriate research for putting it to the test. I believe such definitive research is entirely possible but

> has not yet been done. So all we are left with are various lines of evidence, no one of which is definitive alone, but which, viewed all together, make it a not unreasonable hypothesis that genetic factors are strongly implicated in the average Negro-white intelligence difference. (P. 82)

Thus, studies of Black-White differences in intelligence simply tell us that Black scores tend to be about 15 points below those of Whites. They do not indicate *why* such a consistent discrepancy exists, and one logically could infer the differences as being due to heredity or environment or the interaction between the two. This investigator agrees with Jensen that all possible reasons for the discrepancy should be examined. Therefore, the possibly environmental factors should be mentioned.

The Case for the Environmentalists

When one speaks of "environment," it should be recognized that this concept represents "the sum total of the stimulation the individual receives from conception til death" (Anastasi, cited in Samuda, 1975). The environmentalist agrees with the hereditarian that Blacks earn lower scores than do Whites on I.Q. tests but maintains that this result is a function of differential environmental influences, biased tests, or both. In 1943, Biesheuvel, after reviewing all of the research on the subject up to that time, stated, "By means of a number of carefully conducted investigations, it has been established beyond all doubt that numerous environmental influences do materially affect the magnitude of the I.Q." (p. 15). Several subsequent studies giving evidence of substantially increased I.Q.s as a consequence of environmental modification seem to verify additionally the role of environmental influences (e.g., Davis, 1947; Skodak & Skeels, 1949; Garber & Heber, 1977; Lewin, 1977). In one such study, Garber and Heber (1977), after determining that the greatest predictor of a child's I.Q. is the I.Q. of the mother, studied 40 infants and children, aged three months to six years, whose mothers had I.Q.s of 75 or less as measured by the Wechsler Adult Intelligence Scale. Of the 40 children, 20 were assigned to an experimental group and the remaining 20 were used as controls. The experimental group received infant stimulation and (for the older children) both language skills and problem solving experiences. There was also a remedial and skills training program for the mothers of the experimental group. A follow-up study eight years later showed that the mean WISC I.Q. of the experimental group was 110 as opposed to a mean of 80 for the control group.

Specific environmental factors that have been shown to influence I.Q. score are social class and amount of schooling (Pyle, 1979), as well as self-concept, motivation, test sophistication, and language (Samuda, 1975). More recently discovered variables in this regard are family size and birth order: Individuals from large families tend to have lower I.Q.s than those from smaller families and vice versa. Also, those born late in the sibling line appear to have lower I.Q.s than those born earlier (Pyle, 1979). Because Blacks tend to have larger families than Whites, the often observed Black-White difference in intelligence test scores actually may not be racial at all but merely a distinction related to family size, birth order, and birth interval (Chance, 1975). Recognizing the wide range of contributing sociocultural factors, Pyle (1979) states that:

> Any definition of intelligence must take into account the culture in which an individual is reared. That is, intelligence is inextricably interwoven with the beliefs, values, language, concepts and orientations of a particular group of race of people. We often refer to a range of skills valued by one community at a particular time and virtually assume that the whole world holds similar values. . . . It makes no sense to speak of intelligence in isolated ways, and attempts to divorce intelligence from the culture in which an individual is living are doomed from the start. (P. 6)

Significantly, Biesheuvel (1943), after attempting to compare the intelligence of Africans and Europeans, and after recognizing an inability to control environmental factors, concluded that his research points inevitably to but one conclusion: "That under present circumstances, and by means of the usual techniques, the difference between the intellectual capacity of Africans and Europeans cannot scientifically be determined" (p. 191). Biesheuvel was highly critical of researchers who do not hold to the highest standards of precision and who present as scientific findings that which results from rough approximations of scientific rigor, with the excuse that more precise methods are not available. Accordingly, he felt that rather than conduct partially scientific research, "a problem should be left alone until precise methods of dealing with it are found" (p. 19).

Within recent years, the charge of test bias seems to have become more vocal than the criticism of differential environmental influences. After examining a wide range of publications on the uses and misuses of tests with Black children, Williams (1972) concluded that "the traditional ability tests systematically and consistently lead to assigning of improper and false labels on Black children, and consequently to dehumanization and Black intellectual genocide" (p. 77). This means that these tests are not valid for Black children, since validity refers to "the extent to which the test measures what it is intended to measure" (Williams, p. 79).

One of the most widely used tests for the measurement of children's I.Q. is the Wechsler Intelligence Scale For Children (WISC), which included no Blacks in the original standardization group (Wechsler, 1949). Although Blacks were included in the revised edition of 1974 (WISC-R), the original WISC is still being used to assess the intelligence of Black children. Both the original WISC and the WISC-R consist of five Verbal Tests and five Performance Tests. The five Verbal Tests, each consisting of between 14 and 32 items, are identified as Information, Comprehension, Arithmetic, Similarities, and Vocabulary. There also is a Digit Span Test which serves as a "spare." The Performance Tests are all nonverbal and are designated as Picture Arrangement, Picture Completion, Block Design, Object Assembly, and Coding. The Mazes Test serves as the "spare" for the Performance Tests. From the administration of the entire scale, three I.Q.s are obtained: a Verbal I.Q., a Performance I.Q., and a Full Scale I.Q. Based on the normal distribution curve, the following I.Q. classifications have been established for the Wechsler Scales (Wechsler, 1949; 1955; 1974):

Classification	*I.Q.*
Mental Defective	Below 70
Borderline	70 to 79
Dull Normal (Low Average)	80 to 89
Average	90 to 109
Bright Normal (High Average)	110 to 119
Superior	120 to 129
Very Superior	Above 129

For the WISC-R, 49.4 percent of the sample had I.Q.s between 90 and 109, 16.2 percent were between 80 and 89, and 6 percent scored between 70 and 79, while 2.2 percent fell below 69. For high average, superior, and very superior, the percentages were 16.5, 7.4, and 2.3 respectively.

As examples of invalidity within the original WISC are several items on the Comprehension Test. One of these items asks what the child would do if sent to buy a loaf of bread and told by the grocer that there was no more bread. Within the context of White middle-class experience, the correct response would be to go to another store. However, in many inner-city neighborhoods, a number of families establish credit with the local grocer and obtain food items whenever needed, with the understanding that the merchant is to be paid at periodic intervals, based on the due-date of the major wage earner's paycheck. The child from such a household would be acting most intelligently if he or she returned home after learning that the grocer had no more bread. To go to another store with no money certainly would not be very bright. But even if the child is given money for the purchase, there are cultural factors which may preclude his going to another store. In many urban environments, particularly in large cities, there is much rivalry and warfare among male youth gangs. These conflicts involve the protection of rigidly established territorial boundaries. If the only other store is located across the boundary on someone's else's "turf," only a suicidal wish would cause one to consider such an errand. On the same Comprehension Test there is a question about "correct" behavior when one sees a train approaching a broken track. A respondent who says "get the heck out of there" would receive no credit. Yet, according to his or her conditioned experiences of juvenile arrests based on very weak evidence, running away might represent plain "common sense."

Even on the Performance Tests of the original WISC one finds a cultural bias. For example, the Picture Arrangement Test requires that the subject arrange a series of pictures in the correct sequence of events. This writer, while administering the test to a Black child, noticed that she failed one of the items. Since the items are arranged in increasing order of difficulty, she would be expected to fail in the succeeding item also, in which case the test would be discontinued. However, she not only passed the next item but also earned maximum bonus points for speed. The item related to growing corn and taking it to market. When I asked her why she was able to complete the item so quickly, she smiled annd replied, "I used to live on a farm." This clearly indicated that her success on that item was due to familiarity with the overall cultural context from which the item was taken and implied that her failures may have been due to a related unfamiliarity; hence, intellectual ability may not have been measured at all. Significantly, a basic assumption of I.Q. testing is that all subjects have had equal opportunities for exposure to the test content. One might ask by what reasoning would the opportunity for exposure to matters of farming be equal for the urban dweller and the rural dweller? Certainly their divergent experiences cause differential perceptions which become an important function in their responses to test stimuli. This factor may be equally critical for both the Performance and Verbal Tests, since virtually all of the tests involve perceptual organization. Ironically, familiarity with the social context from which the item is taken can militate *against* the examinee, particularly when the "correct" answer is based on a stereotype and the examinee's response is based on actual experience. In administering the original Wechsler Adult Intelligence Scale (WAIS) to adolescent males at a correctional institution in New Jersey, this author discovered that the inmates consistently "failed" on the Picture Arrangement item labeled "Hold Up." In the "correct" arrangement, the card showing the defendant behind bars is placed *after* the card showing him in court. The inmates, however, placed the in-jail card *before* the in-court card, reflecting their actual experiences and causing them to have their responses recorded as failures. All of these inmates were serving sentences subsequent to court conviction and certainly knew the distinction between pretrial and post-sentence incarceration, the functional difference between a jail and a prison. For the general public, it is likely that this distinction is either vague or nonexistent. For example, one often hears television newscasters report that a defendant received "a thirty-year *jail* sentence," thus indicating a widespread misconception regarding the institutions of incarceration to such a degree that the false impression of a jail being a place of detention *after* conviction becomes the "correct" response on a standardized intelligence test. When one examines the cards of the "Hold Up" item more carefully, the pervasiveness of the stereotype becomes striking: the "robber" has a handkerchief over his mouth only, and the incarceration card shows him with a shaven head while wearing a horizontally striped suit. Hence, we see the valid experiences of a cultural minority (correctional inmates) repudiated, their real-life experiences labeled as incorrect, and the lowered I.Q. presented as evidence of innate intellectual deficiency.

In addition to the apparent invalidity of many of the test items are factors in the testing environment which serve to operate deleteriously for the Black examinee. As long ago as 1936, in a study involving the administration of the Stanford Binet to Black and White children, using Black and White examiners, H. G. Canady found that the mean I.Q. was six points higher when the subjects were tested by an examiner of his own race. With a current national proportion of less than 2 percent of Black psychologists, it is possible that a sizable portion of the Black-White disparity in I.Q. might be explained in terms of this racial difference between tester and testee, particularly since Black examinees probably have White examiners while White examinees probably have examiners of their own race.

Also not to be overlooked are the many nongenetic biological factors as pointed out by Pyle (1979): prenatal and perinatal conditions, age of the mother at the time of delivery (mothers who give birth before age 20 and after age 35 stand a greater risk of having retarded offspring), diet of the mother during pregnancy, length of pregnancy, abnormal delivery, etc. Also, the mother's substance abuse and disease state (e.g. German measles) can be related to intellectual deficiencies in the offspring.

With all of these nongenetic factors operating usually in either an uncontrolled or a poorly controlled fashion, Jensen's 1969 conclusion that 80 percent of the I.Q. score is determined by genetic factors becomes curious indeed. Most scientists disagree with the hereditarian view of intelligence not only on theoretical, philosophical, and logical grounds but also because of the poor evidence in support of this biological argument (Kamin, 1974; Pyle, 1979). If one were to take into consideration, in a controlled fashion, all of the environmental and other nongenetic variables relating to I.Q., the 15-point difference between Blacks and Whites might be obliterated completely. The inability of present knowledge to control all of the relevant variables may provide cause for frustration and skepticism but certainly does not provide scientific evidence for concluding a primarily genetic basis for intelligence.

Because of the continued use of traditional I.Q. tests for the assessment and classification of minority children in the public schools, in spite of the apparent biases and questionable validity involved, a class action suit was filed in the state of California in 1971 to prohibit such testing. This was the first case of its kind in the United States, and its results may have a profound impact throughout the country. The developments in the case, according to Dent (1980), were as follows:

1. The *Larry P.* case was a class action suit brought by a group of six Black parents in San Francisco whose children had been inappropriately classified and placed in classes for the educable mentally retarded (EMR) in the San Francisco Unified School District.
2. The suit was filed in the U.S. District Court for the Northern

District of California on November 24, 1971 (No. C-71-2270 FRP), naming as defendants the California State Superintendent of Public Instruction, the members of the California State Board of Education, the Superintendent of Schools for the San Francisco Unified School District, and the members of the San Francisco Board of Education.

3. The suit contended that civil rights of the children, guaranteed by the Fourteenth Amendment of the Constitution, had been violated and that they had been denied equal opportunity to education as guaranteed by the Civil Rights Act of 1964 and the California Education Code.

4. The plaintiffs alleged:
   a. That their children had been inappropriately classified and placed in EMR classes;
   b. That their children represented a class of "all Black children in the state wrongly labelled and retained in EMR classes;"
   c. That the plaintiffs' children and the class they represented had never been mentally retarded but had been wrongfully placed in EMR classes by reason of utilization by school districts throughout the state of standardized I.Q. tests which fail to account for their (plaintiffs' children) cultural background and home experiences;
   d. That testing procedures are authorized and required by the California State Department of Education;
   e. That EMR classes are authorized by the California Education Code;
   f. That pursuant to the California Education Code (section 6902), such classes should be designed to make EMR students "economically useful and socially adjusted."

5. The use of culturally biased I.Q. tests results in a disproportionately large number of Black children being wrongly labelled mentally retarded and inappropriately placed in EMR classes.

   For example: In 1969, 28.5 percent of the students enrolled in the San Francisco Unified School District were Black, but 58 percent of the students in EMR classes in San Francisco were Black. In the same year, 9.1 percent of all students in public schools in the State of California were Black, but 27.5 percent of all students in EMR classes in the state were Black.

6. The data for state enrollment in 1973 was essentially the same

as it was in 1969, 9 percent of the public school students were Black, 25 percent of those in EMR classes were Black. However, actual numbers of students in EMR classes in the state had decreased markedly, from almost 55,000 in 1969 to 34,000 in 1973. The proportions remained the same.

7. At the other end of the continuum there was a disproportionately small number of Black children enrolled in the classes for Mentally Gifted Minors (MGM). In 1969 the State Department of Education reported that only 2.5 percent of the children in MGM classes were Black, yet 9 percent of the children in public schools were Black.

8. On June 21, 1972, Judge Robert F. Peckham issued a preliminary injunction against the San Francisco Unified School District to enjoin the district from requiring the use of I.Q. tests that do not account for the cultural and experiential background of Black children.

9. The San Francisco Unified School District appealed that injunction. In August 1973 the Ninth Circuit Court of Appeals upheld Peckham's decision.

10. The plaintiffs went back to court and asked Judge Peckham to extend his injunction to the State of California on behalf of all Black children inappropriately placed in EMR classes.

11. On December 14, 1974, Judge Peckham extended the class of children to include all Black children in the State of California (inappropriately classified EMR) and enjoined the state from requiring the use of culturally biased I.Q. tests for the purpose of placing Black children in EMR classes.

12. The California State Board of Education, at its December meeting, declared a moratorium on the use of I.Q. tests on *all* children being considered for EMR placement.

13. The actual *Larry P.* trial began October 11, 1977, and final arguments were heard on May 30, 1978. Among the witnesses for the plaintiffs were ABPsi members: Asa Hilliard, Ed.D., Reginald Jones, Ph.D., Gerald West, Ph.D., William Pierce, Ph.D., and Harold E. Dent, Ph.D. Other expert witnesses called by the plaintiffs included: Gloria Powell, M.D., Alice Watson, Ph.D., Jane Mercer, Ph.D., George Albee, Ph. D., and Leon Kamin, Ph.D.

14. Defense witnesses included: Lloyd Humphreys, Ph.D., Robert

Thorndike, Ph.D., Leo Monday, Ph.D., and Jerome Doppelt, Ph.D.

15. Almost a year and a half after closing arguments (October 16, 1979), Judge Peckham issued his landmark decision (No. C-71-2270 RFP). The Court found:
    a. That Federal and State Constitutional law and statutory law had been violated (The Civil Rights Act of 1964, Section 504 of the Rehabilitation Act of 1973, and the Education for all Handicapped Children's Act of 1975);
    b. That I.Q. tests were culturally biased and had not been validated for the purpose for which they were being used, placement of Black children in EMR classes;
    c. That the plaintiffs' constitutional rights to equal education had been violated by wrongfully confining them to "dead end" EMR classes;
    d. That the plaintiffs' constitutional guarantees of equal protection by the law had been violated by the State's ". . . unjustified toleration of disproportionate enrollments of Black children in EMR classes, and the use of placement mechanisms, particularly IQ tests, that perpetuate those disproportions. . ." (p. 3);
    e. That "Defendants conduct in connection with the history of IQ testing and special education in California, reveals an unlawful segregative intent. This intent was not necessarily to hurt Black children, but it was an intent to assign a grossly disproportionate number of Black children to the special EMR classes, and it was manifested, *inter alia,* in the use of unvalidated and racially and culturally biased placement criteria" (pp. 3–4).

16. The Court ordered the following injunctive relief:
    a. "Defendants are enjoined from utilizing, permitting the use of, or approving the use of any standardized intelligence test . . . for the identification of Black EMR children or their placement into EMR classes, without securing approval of the Court" (p. 104).
    b. "Defendants are hereby ordered to monitor and eliminate disproportionate placement of Black children in California's EMR classes" (p. 105).
    c. "To remedy the harm to Black children who have been misidentified as EMR pupils and to prevent these discriminatory practices from recurring in California with respect to a similarly

situated class of youngsters in the future, the defendants shall direct each school district to reevaluate every Black child currently identified as an EMR pupil, without including in the psychological evaluation a standardized intelligence or ability test, that has not been approved by the court. . . ." (pp. 106–107).

17. In December 1979 the California State Board of Education voted *not* to appeal the *Larry P.* decision.
18. Wilson Riles, the California State Superintendent of Public Instruction, announced he would appeal the *Larry P.* decision.

In clarification of this last point, it seems that Mr. Riles was able to appeal independently of and in opposition to the State Board of Education's general agreement, because he was a separately named defendant. Officially ruling on this appeal, the California Appellate Court decided to uphold Judge Peckham's original determination (H. E. Dent, personal communication, November 13, 1989).

Culture-Specific, Culture-Free, and Culture-Fair Tests of Intelligence

Most standardized I.Q. tests in use today are culture-specific in that they are comprised of items and validated against responses taken from the specific culture of the White middle class. Hence, persons belonging to other socioeconomic classes and other racial groups tend to make responses that deviate from the identified norm. As a means of correcting for this bias, some investigators have suggested that separate intelligence tests should be developed for minority groups. As a consequence, Adrian Dove, in 1966, developed the Counterbalance General Intelligence Test and Robert L. Williams produced the Black Intelligence Test of Cultural Homogeneity, in 1972. Both of these instruments are specific to Black culture and therefore are composed of material that is unfamiliar to most middle-class Whites. The Williams test is a 100-item, multiple-choice test consisting of words and phrases taken from the Black experience. Though not yielding an actual I.Q., the results are helpful in determining the degree of an individual's familiarity with Black values, traditions, customs, and overall world-view, as reflected in the vocabulary of Black culture.

It has been argued by some that culturally specific tests should be devised for each major group in the United States (Samuda, 1975). However, such an undertaking would be not only financially prohibitive but also questionable in terms of positive applicability in the larger society, since the test results cannot be generalized beyond the specific culture for which the test is developed (Samuda, 1975).

A logical solution to the dilemma created by the cultural relativity of traditional intelligence test scores would be to develop a culturally uncontaminated or "culture-free" instrument. Such a device would represent "an attempt at stripping the individual of his cultural veneer in order to reveal and expose his true and inherent abilities" (Samuda, 1975, p. 133). In other words, remove the nurture and expose the nature "which lies buried in pure from deep in the individual" (Wesman, cited in Samuda, p. 133). After some attempts, investigators recognized that "a culture-free test was simply an impossibility" (Samuda, p. 133), and the focus shifted to the development of "culture-fair" tests. Such tests require materials, aptitudes, and skills that, selectively and restrictively, are common to *all* cultures. Again, no such test either exists or seems possible to develop (Anastasi, 1968). On this point Anastasi states:

> no one test can be universally applicable or equally "fair" to all cultures . . . it is unlikely that any test can be equally "fair" to more than one cultural group, especially if the norms are quite dissimilar. . . . Every test tends to favor persons from the culture in which it was developed. . . . Each culture encourages and fosters certain abilities and ways of behaving, and discourages or suppresses others. It is therefore to be expected that, on tests developed within the American culture, Americans will generally excel. If a test were constructed by the same procedures within a culture differing markedly from ours, Americans would probably appear deficient in terms of test norms. Data bearing on this type of cultural comparison are meager. What evidence is available, however, suggests that persons from our culture may be just as handicapped on tests prepared within other cultures as members of those cultures are on our tests. (P. 251)

An alternative might be to develop a measure comprised of items which are common to *many* cultures, as validated against local criteria (Anastasi, 1982), and it is within this purview that the designation "culture-fair" currently is assigned.

In this regard, several culture-fair tests have been developed within recent years and have been described comprehensibly (Samuda, 1975; Sweetland and Keyser, 1983). Another recently produced instrument that has been well-received as a culture-fair measure is the Kaufman

Assessment Battery for Children, also known as the K-ABC (Wortman and Loftus, 1988). As Wortman and Loftus indicate, this test reduces the effect of language ability on the test taker's performance. Hence, what is evaluated is closer to pure problem solving-skill. The test also "tries to separate problem solving ability from performance based on the amount of knowledge a youngster has acquired" (Wortman and Loftus, 1988, p. 390). Moreover, the K-ABC "produces a gap between the mean scores for Black and White youngsters that is less than half the gap associated with traditional IQ tests" (Klanderman, Devine and Mollner, cited in Wortman and Loftus, 1988, p. 390).

In spite of such encouraging developments, some psychologists have questioned the need for an enhanced focus on culture-fair tests. The argument is that traditional I.Q. tests actually do predict school grades and success on the job for all test takers, minority and nonminority alike. Hence, according to this viewpoint, those who do not perform well on the tests are deficient in skills that are important in our society. Thus, a lively debate has developed regarding the desirability of culture-fair over culture-specific tests of intelligence.

Fortunately, more promising points of concentration have been indicated by the Pluralistic Evaluation technique of Jane Mercer (1973, 1979), the Instrumental Enrichment approach of Reuven Feuerstein (1979), and the Structure of Intellect focus of Mary Meeker (1963). Mercer's system compares individuals within their own sociocultural backgrounds and does not classify them as intellectually deficient unless they score within the lowest three percent for their own sociocultural group. She has found that minority children earn about the same scores as middle-class children when this sociocultural factor is equal and that "minority children whose families are least like the dominant culture receive scores that relegate them to the borderline of mental retardation" (Samuda, 1975, p. 143). As an aid in her assessment, Mercer has created the System of Multicultural Pluralistic Assessment (SOMPA), which is available commercially.

Feuerstein's Instrumental Enrichment approach involves four to five hours of assessment and teaching, all at one time and usually without a break. It is essentially a test-teach-test situation involving progressively complex tasks, wherein the examiner is active, directive, and instructive, while carefully noting the concepts and tasks that the child does not understand. To assist in the evaluation and teaching of the child, Feuerstein has developed the Learning Potential Assessment Device (LPAD), which, like Mercer's SOMPA, is available commercially, but only for those specifically trained in its use.

Mary Meeker's method, based on the work of J. P. Guilford, assesses and classifies intelligence along three dimensions, each of which is composed of several subdivisions. These dimensions and subdivisions are measured by means of the Structure of Intellect test (SOI) and are used to analyze and improve areas of weakness. The SOI is available from the SOI Institute in California. It is important to note that while the Mercer approach is one primarily of assessment, the methods of Feuerstein and Meeker involve both assessment and training for improvement, thus indicating that the I.Q. can be enhanced. Given the currently strong criticism of traditional I.Q. tests, the relatively successful methods of Meeker and Feuerstein may shape the future course of intelligence testing worldwide. Feuerstein's approach and theory, for example, are being applied not only in his native Israel but also in Venuezuela and the United States (Chance, 1981).

Groups with Above Average I.Q.s

As recently pointed out by Williams (1984), a major limitation of both hereditarian and environmentalist research is that they focus solely on those groups, usually racial and ethnic minorities, who consistently fall below the White I.Q. norm and ignore those groups whose mean scores regularly surpass this norm. Research on these intellectually "superior" groups might assist us in our attempts to understand the degree to which hereditary and environmental factors contribute to the I.Q.

A recent study of the Japanese I.Q. by Lynn (1982) has underscored the value of such an approach. Lynn sampled 1100 Japanese children with the Performance Test of the WISC-R, testing 100 subjects in each age group from 6 through 16, and found that the Japanese mean was 111, as opposed to the United States mean of 100. He reported that this performance represents the highest showing among the developed nations of the world, since subjects in Britain, France, Belgium, Germany, Australia, and New Zealand all have mean I.Q.s that are about the same as the United States mean. Fully 70 percent of the Japanese have a higher I.Q. than the average European or American, and 10 percent have I.Q.s over 130, as opposed to 2 percent for Americans. The specific tests on which the Japanese performed best were Block Design, Mazes, Picture Arrangement, and Object Assembly. A further finding was that the Japanese I.Q. has been rising almost steadily since the end of World War II, as evidenced by previous studies with the WISC and the WAIS. These studies reveal the correlation between I.Q. and year of birth to be .76 and statistically significant. Obviously, this rise in national I.Q. cannot be attributed to a modification in the genetic structure of the population and must be due to environmental changes, possibly improvements in health and nutrition. However, this increase could be related also to the increased proportion of Japanese students who continue their education past junior high school, the possibility that Japanese children have been more highly conditioned to taking exams, and the early training in visual relationships that the complex Japanese alphabet provides (Mohs, 1982).

The Scholastic Aptitude Test

Closely related to the controversy and conflict over Black I.Q. scores is the matter of Black performance on the College Board's Scholastic Aptitude Test (SAT), especially since many academicians and other professionals in the field of higher education view the SAT score as an absolute measure of one's intellect. The sanctity of the score often persists even in the presence of unquestionably contravening evidence. McClelland (1973) points out that admissions personnel often view test scores as being actually more valid than the behavior criterion, reporting that "it is amazing to me how often my colleagues say things like: 'I don't care how well he can write; just look at these test scores'" (p. 10). Although McClelland's observation referred to test scores for graduate school admission, recent reports indicate that decision makers at the undergraduate level have similar attitudes regarding the Scholastic Aptitude Test.

Undeniably, the mean SAT scores for Blacks, on both the Verbal and Mathematics sections of the test, tend to fall below those of Whites to a statistically significant degree. But as with the discussion regarding the I.Q., the serious researcher should seek to discover *why* such differences exist. Before this question is raised, however, it is necessary to establish that the measuring instrument actually gauges what it purports to assess; otherwise, the score will have little meaning. As pointed out earlier, a test which in fact measures what it professes to measure is said to possess *validity*. If this valid measuring is done consistently, the instrument would be regarded as having *reliability*. However, validity and reliability are continuous rather than discrete, and may be determined by means of correlation coefficients. The detailed explanations of the specific procedures involved in the computations of these coefficients, kindred to the earlier discussion of correlation, are beyond the scope of this volume, but may be investigated further through the formal study of statistical methods and procedures. Also, as with the explanation of correlation earlier in this chapter, validity and reliability coefficients may vary between +1.00 and −1.00. However, because of selection factors, these coefficients almost always are positive. In the case of validity, the score on the test in question is correlated with a criterion measure, which could be another test.

For reliability, three general approaches have been recognized. In one procedure, the test-retest technique, an individual's performance on one administration of the test is compared with his or her showing on a second administration of the same test. Another approach, the two-form procedure, correlates the score earned on one form of the test with that obtained on a parallel form of the test. A third method, the split-half procedure, relates the performance on one half of the test to the results on the second half of the test.

Attempts to determine the extent to which the SAT measures what it purports to measure were made as early as 1932 and have continued until the present. The research since 1964 indicates that for students in general and with college grade-point average (GPA) as the criterion measure, SAT scores tend to add only about 8 percent prediction to what is foretold by high school rank (HSR) *alone* (Slack & Porter, 1980). These authors also show that correlating SAT with all three predictors simultaneously (SAT-Verbal, SAT-Math, and HSR) yields a coefficient (R^2) of about .58. This means that 58 percent of the variance in college GPA is attributable to the combination of HSR and SAT and that 42 percent is related to other factors. More importantly, Slack and Porter found that 50 percent of the total variance was due to HSR *alone*, leaving the aforementioned 8 percent ascribable to SAT. For minority students, the proportion of variance owing to SAT is also 8 percent, but the amount chargeable to HSR is much lower, resulting in an overall coefficient between .22 and .36 (Houston, 1980, 1983). Thus, for minorities, 64 to 78 percent of the variance in college GPA is derivable from factors other than the three predictors. The fact that virtually all validity studies show the SAT to contribute a maximum of only 8 percent to the variance in GPA is at odds with the claim by the Educational Testing Service that "countless studies" show the SAT to be "almost invariably effective in predicting academic success" (Slack & Porter, 1980, p. 165). Slack and Porter state that "when we examined these 'countless studies' we were unable to unearth a basis for the claim that the SAT is an effective predictor" (p. 165). After careful review of all available evidence, the authors concluded that "contrary to the conclusions of ETS and the College

Board, students can raise their scores with training, the scores are not a good predictor of college performance and the test does not measure 'capacity' to learn" (p. 155).

In view of the relative invalidity of the SAT, it is not surprising that, in spite of comparatively low entrance examination scores, minority students have performed quite well, academically, in our nation's colleges and universities, including those of highest prestige (Boyd, 1977). Yet, admissions officers and faculty members regard the SAT not only as a valid predictor of college success but also as a measure of overall intellectual worth. For example, Stipp (1985) reveals that in spite of the current evidence that the SAT is a poor measure of academic skills, the test curiously carries more influence today than ever before, and the number of colleges using it is at an all-time high. The test has become not only a gauge of student competence but also a criterion of institutional quality and prestige, and many admissions officers worry that, like those of football coaches, their very jobs may depend upon their ability to attract high scorers. That this fear is not unfounded is underscored by the report of one admissions director in California who reported that he was forced to resign because he recruited too many students with low SAT scores (Stipp, 1985).

However, the recent decision by Bates College (in Lewiston, Maine) to discontinue the SAT as an admissions requirement and the possibility that Harvard may do the same (Stipp, 1985) is a sign that there is developing a change in sentiment, which may result in widespread reassessment of the value of present-day testing for college admission.

One potentially promising approach to this problem is to seek nonacademic predictors of college achievement, such as motivation, academic interest, and study skills. In a recent preliminary investigation of the relationship between study skills and grade-point average, (Houston, 1987) the author analyzed a study skills questionnaire which was administered to a sample of 83 White male and female undergraduates at a large university in the Northeast. The results showed that of eight study skills variables, only one (time management) was significantly correlated with college grade-point average. If similar results are obtained with Blacks, we will have a predictor of college achievement which, when combined with high school rank, will be superior to the predictability of the Scholastic Aptitude Test. When this time management predictor was added to high school rank, the accuracy of prediction was increased by 16 percent. This result is in contrast to the 8 percent accuracy increase obtained when both the verbal and the math sections of the Scholastic Aptitude Test are added to high school rank. If these results are upheld in future research, a major value will be not simply the discovery of a measure to replace the Scholastic Aptitude Test, but the potential for devising time management programs for college students and potential college students, in order to increase their chances of success in higher education.

CHAPTER SIX
Frustration and Adjustment

> Sometimes I feel like nothin', somethin' throwed away; then I get my guitar and play the blues all day. (Blues Ballad)

Frustration has been defined by Webster's Third International Dictionary (1971) as "a deep, chronic sense or condition of insecurity, discouragement, and dissatisfaction arising from thwarted drives, inner conflicts or other unresolved problems." Human adjustment involves developing the adaptations and modifications that are necessary for dealing with this source of tension.

As Symonds (1949) has pointed out, frustrations are not rare occurrences which accompany misfortune. Rather, they are being continually produced, and the organism ceaselessly is required to restore the disturbance in equilibrium caused by the blocking of various needs. Thus, the individual must exert effort towards reducing the frustration. One exception to this basic principle is the need for oxygen, which is satisfied automatically by the breathing reflex. Many frustrations are minor, and cause little concern, while others are so severe that they may threaten the organism or result in personality disorganization. On the basis of the primary source, frustration can be classified into three general types: *personal frustration, conflict frustration, and environmental frustration* (Ruch, 1963).

Personal frustration arises when the individual is thwarted by a real or imagined personal liability, which may be either physical or psychological. Thus, the high school student who aspires to attend college but fails to achieve the minimum SAT score, the college football player whose lack of skill causes him to be bypassed by a scout from the National Football League, and the eager applicant who fails to meet the physical requirements of the police academy all may experience personal frustration. They perceive themselves as being personally deficient in the relevant requirements necessary for the attainment of their goal. Thus, personal frustration tends to result in feelings of inferiority, which often reinforce the frustration, causing a vicious cycle.

Environmental frustration originates from aspects of the physical or social environment. Experiencing a flat tire on a heavily traveled shoulderless narrow highway in the middle of the "rush hour," flunking an academic course, witnessing rain at a picnic, or being fired from a job are examples of this type of frustration.

Conflict frustration results when one must choose between two equally strong motives or goals, as when a student must decide whether to study or to attend a party. Since she cannot do both simultaneously, she is in conflict. Realistically, everyone probably experiences some degree of frustration, at least some of the time.

Factors Determining the Degree of Frustration

As indicated above, frustration results from the thwarting of desires or needs. However, these needs may be physical or psychological and the intensity of the frustration varies according to several factors (Dollard et al., 1939; Symonds, 1949). One such factor is the motivational level of the individual. A person whose hunger is intense will show greater frustration regarding an eating obstacle than will a person whose hunger is relatively weak, if all other factors are equal. Another factor is the strength of the barrier. The stronger the barrier, the greater will be the frustration and vice versa. An adolescent in a rigidly authoritarian household who is told that she must return home from the party at twelve midnight will be more frustrated than the one from a relatively democratic home who is given the same curfew.

A third factor is the number of frustrated response sequences the individual has endured. This often is referred to as the "cumulative effect" and indicates that the degree of frustration experienced at any given time is a function of the amount of unresolved frustration experienced in the past. Thus, the frustration tends to accumulate until the person endures "the last straw," which might be of even lower magnitude than any other contributing frustrations.

A fourth determinant of the degree of frustration is the availability of substitutes. If alternate means of gaining the required gratification are available, the frustration will be reduced in intensity. The high school senior who has varying chances of being accepted by several colleges can rank-order her choices with the likelihood of at least some gratification. On the other hand, the applicant who can hope to enter only one college would suffer much more pain if she were denied admission.

Finally, frustration is relative to the amount of security and emotional support one can gain. A serious student who fails to score a passing grade on an exmaination certainly would be frustrated. But the frustration is less distressing when it is learned that many other students also failed. The old adage "misery loves company" might be appropriate here.

Reactions to Frustration

When frustration is encountered, the individual at first attempts, by means of some direct effort, to remove or reduce the distress. These direct responses are aggression, realistic hard work, the development of new skills, and reinterpretation of the situation. Many of these approaches are used by mental health practitioners to assist persons who require help with problems of adjustment.

Aggression

One of the most immediate responses to frustration is that of aggression, which is an attempt forcefully to overcome the barrier by attacking and/or inflicting injury. Some investigators have suggested not only that aggression always is the result of frustration, but also that frustration always leads to some form of aggression (Dollard et al., 1939). This view has been regarded as extreme, and subsequently was modified by the original authors. However, since most societies prohibit the raw expression of aggression, most individuals find other forms of direct action.

Realistic Hard Work

Without necessarily resorting to aggression, the organism may work persistently at overcoming the barrier. The basketball player who lacks ability in foul shooting may practice for hours until he improves. The adolescent unable to locate a suitable date for the prom may serch indefatigably until a partner is found. The applicant for the state police force who discovers that he is a few pounds underweight may undergo a body-building regimen until he attains the minimum poundage.

The Development of New Skills

Often merely "working hard" at overcoming a barrier may be unrewarding, since repeating ineffective responses often is quite futile.

Hence, it sometimes is necessary to cultivate a new skill. The poor foul shooter may find it necessary to hold the ball differently, to aim for the back of the rim instead of the front, or to use the backboard as a pivot. The individual seeking a date may find it more satisfying to develop a less aversive and more polished approach, and the police applicant may discover that he should do something other than 40 daily pushups to accomplish his goal.

Reinterpreting the Situation

Another means of resolving frustration directly is to reassess and retranslate the situation so as to form an alternate and less stressful perception. The parents of an adolescent may be frustrated because of "evidence" that their teenage son is becoming disrespectful and rejecting; he criticizes and argues with them, is disobedient, and spends increasingly more time away from the home. A reevaluation of the picture might reveal that the "criticism" is really an attempt, out of devotion to and love for his parents, to improve his family maximally; that the arguing and disobedience are normal adolescent quests for assertion and independence; that the time spent away from the home represents average teenage peer-group associatons, and so on. Accordingly, such reinterpretation may cause a marked diminution in frustration.

Defense Mechanisms

If direct approaches are unsuccessful, the individual may resort to more indirect methods. Such approaches, also referred to as detour behavior, are characterized primarily by the *defense mechanisms,* those techniques, unconsciously constructed and implemented, which serve to defend the individual against the anxiety that might result from non-gratification. These devices are known also as ego defenses and dynamisms. The most common of these specific adjustment devices are repression, sublimation, compensation, overcompensation, rationalization, projection, identification, regression, reaction formation, fantasy, and denial. The definitions of these mechanisms found below are taken from Plutchik et al. (1979), but the examples are those of the present author.

Repression

Repression is the exclusion from consciousness of an idea and its associated emotions, or an experience and its associated emotions. This technique is said to be the most important of the defense mechanisms because according to Anna Freud (cited in Hinsie & Campbell, 1970), "the other mechanisms have only to complete what repression has left undone, or to deal with such prohibitied areas as return to consciousness when repression fails." Repression also has been referred to as selective forgetting, since the individual is motivated unconsciously to block out certain experiences from memory (Goleman, Egen, & Davids, 1982). The otherwise unexplained forgetting of names, dates, faces, skills, or even one's own identity can be caused by repression.

Compensation

Compensation is an intensive attempt to correct or find a suitable substitute for a real or imagined physical or psychological inadequacy For example, a student unconsciously may experience feelings of inferiority in dealing with academic subject matter. In order to correct for the perceived inferiority, and remain unaware of it, she may excel in athletic endeavors.

Overcompensation

Overcompensation is an intense attempt to correct for a real or imagined physical or psychological inadequacy by showing superiority in the very area in which the inadequacy unconsciously is experienced. An individual who unconsciously regards himself to be inferior academically may actually surpass most other students in academic achievement, thus shielding himself against the painful recognition of the inferiority belief.

Rationalization

This is the use of plausible reasons to justify actions caused by repressed, unacceptable feelings. The individual who fails an examination may attribute the failure to lack of sufficient study, or the baseball player who misses an easy "pop" fly ball may explain that the sun was in his eyes. Although untrue, the explanation cannot be dismissed simply as a lie, because the rationalizer is not aware of the falsity of the misrepresentation.

Identification

This mechanism involves the unconscious modeling of attitudes and behaviors after another person as a way of increasing feelings of self-worth or coping with the possible separation or loss. Probably the most common type of identification is that by children with parents. Typically the boy identifies primarily with the father and the girl principally with the mother. People also identify with heroes, entertainers, sports figures, political figures, etc., thus receiving vicarious gratification from a wide range of needs.

Projection

This device is an unconscious rejection of one's emotionally unacceptable thoughts, traits, or wishes, and the attribution of them to people and things in the outside world. It is important to recognize that this mechanism, being unconscious like all other mechanisms, cause the individual to externalize unacceptable inner material and to view it as having originated "out there" in the thing or person onto which it is projected. Thus, statements like "He's planning to steal the wallet" or "He's going to get her drunk" might reveal more about the producers than the objects of those utterances.

Denial

Here the typical characteristic is a lack of awareness of certain events, experiences, or feelings that it would be painful to acknowledge. Although rejection of unacceptable inner material also is characteristic of projection, in denial this rejection is central and primary. Moreover, additional mechanisms, such as rationalization, may be called into play in support of the denial. Thus, the man who denies his overweight condition may argue, if reality is presented to him, that the scale is broken or that the suit shrank.

Sublimation

This particular technique involves gratification of the repressed instinct or unacceptable feeling, particularly sexual or aggressive, by socially acceptable alternatives. The person with unresolved, pent-up hostility may become a surgeon or a professional boxer. This of course is not to suggest that all surgeons or professional boxers are sublimating hostility. Artistic endeavors, such as music and painting, apparently provide means for sublimating a vast scope of needs and drives.

Displacement

This particular defense involves a discharge of pent-up emotions, usually anger, onto objects, animals, or people perceived as less dangerous by the individual than those that originally aroused the emotion. The young girl, angry with her mother, but inhibited from expressing the anger directly, may release the tension indirectly by picking a fight with another girl.

Regression
This approach entails retreat under stress to earlier or more immature patterns of behavior and gratification. A perfectly toilet-trained child may begin to soil herself after having her security threatened by the birth of an infant or sister.

Reaction Formation
This refers to the prevention of the expression of unacceptable desires, particularly sexual or aggressive, by the development or exaggeration of attitudes and behaviors that are oppositional. The male who unconsciously hates his wife may become the doting husband who showers her with affection, or the unconscious hater of minorities may become an intensely vigorous liberal.

One must remember that for all of these defense mechanisms, the motivation and purpose are unconscious. The individual is aware only of the manifest behavior, which he or she views as undisguised.

Sources of Frustration for Blacks

When we consider, historically, the magnitude and duration of racial oppression, it would seem that Blacks as a group experience a disproportionate share of environmental frustration. The various forms and symptoms of racial prejudice, discrimination, and bigotry have served for centuries as barriers to the desired goals of equal opportunity, just treatment, and participation in the American Dream.

An individual unaware of the many subtle manifestations of racial intolerance might relate thwarted desires to self-deficiency, and consequently could experience *personal* frustration. This danger may heighten if increasingly more of the United States population view the overall society as becoming more accepting of Blacks and other minorities. Overtly blatant racial hostility, obviously, is easy to relate to factors external to the self. But how should one view the denied promotion in an Affirmative Action Equal Opportunity employment setting, the rejected mortgage application by a bank that is an "Equal Housing Lender," the unsuccessful search for adequate shelter in a society with open housing laws, or the refused public accommodation in a country where such refusal on the basis of race is illegal?

One's mental health may depend on whether such situations are seen as being personally or environmentally determined, and the fact that much racial discrimination now is recognized as being institutionalized further compounds an already multifarious set of circumstances.

The inability to meet basic physiological and safety needs, due to direct, indirect, and institutionalized racist barriers, certainly causes tremendous stress and tension. There is even further frustration when it is recognized that those who have been placed, democratically, into the highest positions of power and leadership are unsympathetic, insensitive, and often callous regarding the plight of minorities. This poignant perception is illustrated creatively by Gil Scott-Heron (1974) in his poem "Whitey On the Moon." In this poem, the author describes the despair of noticing millions of dollars being spent on the investigation of outer space, while the safety, health, and general well-being of an individual and his family are in severe jeopardy.

It would be virtually impossible in this volume to catalog the entire scope and span of behavior that is symptomatic of racial invidiousness in the United States. However, several specific sources of frustration, resulting from the disfavor in which Blacks are held, should be mentioned. One such source is the category of African physical characteristics such as hair texture, nasal index, lip density, and skin color. As a consequence of pronounced conditioning since the days of the slave trade until the middle of the 1960s, Black Americans had learned to accept Eurocentric standards of beauty and to reject Africentic standards. Malcolm X (1965) reminded us of this disturbing reality when he observed that the colonial powers of Europe portrayed Africa so disapprovingly that African Americans began to develop a negative identity with Africa and actually came to hate Africa. Because (as Malcolm X sees it) it is impossible, in a Black person, for a positive attitude towards oneself to coexist with a negative attitude towards Africa, Blacks in the United States began to hate themselves. Conversely, a positive attitude towards Africa is incompatible with a negative attitude towards oneself. Hence, the development of a positive attitude towards Africa results in the enhancement of one's sense self-esteem and self-concept. Partly as a consequence of constant reminders of this sort, the civil rights movement of the 1960s ushered in a new awareness among African Americans and restored a suppressed pride in Blackness. However, there is some suspicion that this cultural rehabilitation needs to be reinforced (see chapter 3 for a discussion of reinforcement).

Another major source of frustration is the thwarting of the Black male's quest for manhood (Grier & Cobbs, 1968; Asinof, 1970). The Black male has been taught since the days of slavery to be passive, dependent, and unassertive—the exact antithesis of masculinity. The insistence on such obsequious behavior was necessary for the maintenance of the slave system, and those Black men who posed a threat were quickly eliminated. In addition, wholesale punishment often was inflicted on other Blacks as a "lesson" to the entire Black community. In this way, the entire Black community was inveigled into suppressing Black male aggression, since it became a threat to their own well-being. Since, in our society, economic wealth is correlated with manhood and power, we find that, again, the Black man has been denied. This consistent and ubiquitous disavowal of manhood seems to be one the major causes of seething anger among Black males in the United States.

Although the symbolic and systematic castration of the Black male has been a particularly wretched aspect of racism, the victimization of Black women has been even worse (Lerner, 1972). As Lerner sees it, this victimization of the Black woman has taken five forms. First, Black women share in all aspects of the oppression of Blacks in general; second, Black women have been objects of exploitive sex by White men; third, the rape of Black women has been employed as a weapon of terror directed against the entire Black community; fourth, when Black men are prevented, through social taboos and violence, from defending Black women, the oppression of all Blacks is heightened and institutionalized; finally, when Black men are oppressed economically to the extent that they cannot secure steady employment at decent wages, many Black women are deprived of the support of a male breadwinner and must take on added economic burdens (Lerner, 1972, p. 149). Thus, there is a functional relationship among the castration of the Black male, the victimization of the Black female, and the institutionalization of racism.

Black Coping Devices

Although the general methods of dealing with frustration apparently are essentially the same for Blacks and Whites, there are racial differences regarding the sources of frustration, the intensity of frustration, and the usage incidence of the various defense mechanisms. In addition, the uniqueness of the Black experience has occasioned the development of certain racially-specific coping techniques that have no facsimile or replica among Whites.

Repression

Scholars and researchers have pointed out that sanctions against the direct expression of aggression have been more pronounced for the Black male than for the White male and that Black males, therefore, tend to show a greater need to maintain the repression of this forbidden impulse (Clark, 1965; Grier & Cobbs, 1968; Poussaint, 1970). In fact,

Poussaint tells us that this aggression and its repression seem to be central to the present social and psychological difficulties of Blacks in the United States. He reminds us of the pillage of Africa, the slave trade, the psychological and often physical castration of Black male slaves, and the sexual exploitation as well as other degradation of both male and female slaves. He then points out the systematic strategy that was designed and implemented by Whites to prevent any expression of vengeance on the part of Black men and women. As a consequence, the plantation system created and reinforced Black obsequiousness and resulted in a paternalism that was reinforced rigidly. Thus, the Black man became passive, nonassertive, and compliant. This conditioning was highlighted by social codes of conduct that allowed and often required Whites to address (and to refer to) Black men and women as boys and girls, while mandating that Blacks use the tiles of "Mr." and "Mrs." when addressing Whites. Ridiculously, the racial etiquette held that these titles be used even when addressing Whites by their *first* names (e.g., "Miss Anne," "Mister Charlie"). Any Black who, through his behavior, did not comply with this system of programmed inferiority was punished severely; those who did acquiesce were rewarded relatively substantially.

In an additional discussion of the origin of suppressed aggression among Black males, Grier and Cobbs (1968) also trace the behavior to the realities of slavery, where the Black mother attempted to insure her son's survival by defusing his aggressiveness. Such acting-out, being a threat to the entire slave system, would place the son's life in danger. The authors point out that the Black mother of today continues this heritage from slavery, because even currently the Black man cannot become too aggressive without challenging the balance of this complex social system and thereby causing hazard to himself. Considering that a primary role of any mother is to prepare her child for society's requirements, the Black mother simply (though covertly) conditioned the Black boy for his role in life. "What at first seemed a random pattern of mothering has gradually assumed a definite and deliberate, if unconscious, method of preparing a Black boy for his subordinate place in the world" (Grier & Cobbs, 1968, p. 52).

One major manifestation of this conditioned passivity on the part of Black males is "the postal clerk syndrome" (Grier & Cobbs, 1968). This behavior involves what has been described as passivity, nonassertiveness, submission, and ingratiating compliance in relationships with Whites. It is no puzzle that this phenomenon is most prevalent among the middle-class and upper-class Blacks. They are the ones who have the most contact with Whites and therefore have the greatest opportunity not only to be victimized directly but also to have their aggressive urges and fantasies stimulated. In this sense, the nonassertiveness would seem to represent a type of *reaction formation* that protects the individual from recognizing and/or succumbing to his dangerously aggressive impulses. In a somewhat different interpretation of this repression of aggression, Burkey (1978) views it as cynical role-playing and actually representative of a form of rebellion.

However, this persistent and urgently compelling need for Blacks to inhibit aggression seems to have generalized to all emotions, especially in the Black male, so that he has developed a particular nonchalance, a withholding of all emotional response regardless of the direction and nature of the stimulus (Grier & Cobbs, 1968). The result is that in spite of much inner turmoil, the individual presents a continuous facade of serenity. That this facade includes the suppression and repression of all emotions, including love, may have critical ramifications regarding not only Black-White relations but also Black male-female relationships and the relationships of the Black male with members of his immediate family.

Identification

One traditional mechanism for dealing with aggression is identification. Yet Blacks have had relatively limited access to this procedure. Consider the numerous nonminority males who have been able to identify with John Wayne, Billy the Kid, Wyatt Earp, or Audie Murphy. The bravado, pomposity, self-assertion and grandiose bluster of these self-assertive figures doubtlessly have provided vicarious gratification for countless thousands. Although there are those Blacks who do identify with white cowboys and soldiers, the absence of Black models limits the strength and even the process of the identifiction. Yet, we know that there were thousands of Black cowboys and soldiers during the celebrated days of the "Wild West" (Durham & Jones, 1965; Katz, 1973). Tragically, historical exclusion has denied Blacks an opportunity to identify with these heroes, and the important role that Black cowboys played in taming the "Great Frontier" still is not common knowledge among Blacks. Durham and Jones tell us that the Ninth and Tenth Cavalries, completely Black except for commissioned officers, and referred to by Indians as Buffalo Soldiers because of their bushy hair, engaged in military combat with almost all of the Indian nations. Blacks fought against Crazy Horse and his warriors, captured Geronimo, surrounded Billy the Kid when he was trapped in a burning building in New Mexico, stopped settlers from preempting Indian lands in Oklahoma, and rescued Wyoming cattlemen during the Johnson County War (Durham & Jones, 1965).

One can speculate about the motives of Western folklore in general and Hollywood in particular for concealing this factuality, but such suppression certainly served to disallow Blacks access to a major means of dealing with aggressive tension. The resulting accumulation of this disquietude possibly has contributed to the interpersonal and nonpersonal violence among Blacks in racially segregated areas of our cities and towns. However, there are occasions for working through these tensions by identifying with Blacks of less than national-image stature. Reactions of the masses of Blacks to the "riots" of the late 1960s and early 1970s indicated that even the Black middle class, though aloof from direct involvement, tended to sympathize with and give tacit support to the "rioters" (Clark, 1965). For the more oppressed Blacks, the indentification was much stronger. In his account of a prison-yard encounter, Cleaver (1968) mentions that after four days of unrest in Watts, a group of inmates from the Watts area gathered triumphantly in the prison yard and displayed the sort of jubilation that revealed their unmistakably vicarious participation in the uprising that was taking place many miles away in the Watts ghetto. After describing how two of these inmates had slapped each other's palms in an emotional salutation, Cleaver reports:

> Then one low rider, stepping into the center of circle formed by the others, reared back on his legs and swaggered, hunching his belt up with his forearms as he's seen James Cagney and George Raft do in too many gangster movies . . .
>
> "Baby", he said, "they walking in fours and kicking in doors; dropping reds (a barbiturate called red devils) and busting heads; drinking wine and committing crime; shooting and looting; high-siding (having fun at the expense of another) and low riding; setting fires and slashing tires; turning over cars and burning down bars; making Parker mad and making me glad; putting an end to the "go slow" crap and putting sweet Watts on the map—my Black ass is in Folsom this morning, but my Black heart is in Watts!" Tears of joy were rolling from his eyes.
>
> It was a cleansing, revolutionary laugh we all shared, something we have not often had occasion for. (p. 27)

Although Cleaver's reconstruction of the scene involved conscious considerations, it is probable that for the bulk of those prison participants the basic dynamics were below the surface of awareness and therefore classically defensive in nature.

Overcompensation

Much otherwise puzzling behavior can be explained clearly when the various manifestations of overcompensation are recognized. The poverty-level individual who purchases expensive clothing or a very expensive automobile, for example, may be demonstrating a natural tendency to avoid the anxiety which might result from persistent frustration. The frustrated quest for manhood, mentioned earlier, often is dealt with by Blacks in the form of overcompensation. The bustling bravado and nearly suicidal fearlessness found among many young Black males (Seiden, 1970), suggests an exaggerated attempt to demonstrate masculinity. Often, this magnification takes the form of sexual prodigiousness and usually is misinterpreted by the larger society. In January 1986 a nationally televised program on single parent households among Blacks presented the effect of an endless series of complicated causes, most of which relate to prejudice and racism. Rather than seriously analyzing the causes of the problem, the program took an agonizing look at the victims and suggested that their plight was caused by factors indigenous to them or their culture. The fathers of the "fatherless" children were shown merely as irresponsible, shiftless, selfish, and oversexed. There was no attempt to ferret out the root-cause of the behavior. The "documentary" never even hinted that society may have caused the behavior that they found so undesirable. As was pointed out in chapter 1, every effect has several *possible* causes, and the job of the serious investigator is to discover the true cause by systematic elimination. What are all of the possible root-causes of the increased single-sex families among Blacks? Which ones, on the basis of evidence and logical reasoning, can be eliminated from consideration? A well-designed investigation by a serious researcher might provide meaningful answers which could be instrumental in finding a solution. It is possible that the producers of the documentary engaged in avoidance, denial, and victim-blaming as defenses against recognizing the critical issue and indicting the larger society.

Sublimation

As mentioned earlier, the arts provide fertile ground for the sublimation of tension. For Blacks, musical expression seems to have provided a special means of socially acceptable indirect expression. During slavery, this mode of expression was virtually the only form of ventilation permitted and actually was encouraged by slave masters as a means of avoiding violent rebellion or suicide among the slaves. Music therefore was heard in every aspect of slave life—in the fields, in the slave quarters, and in the church (Comer, 1972). The church, being the one place where large numbers of Blacks could congregate safely, became the germination of the Negro spiritual songs, which often expressed a feeling of despondency and dejection arising from unjust treatment. Since Black music was sanctioned explicitly, it became a means of survival as well as a medium for entertainment. That the structure of this music is rooted in Africa has been well documented by King (1975) and Johnson and Johnson (1925). Present-day Black music derives from this heritage and continues its tension-releasing role. Lomax and Lomax (1947) point out the deep sorrow, the biting irony, and the noble yearning for a better world that is characteristic of Black folk music. One can imagine the pain and suffering that is sublimated when one sings (as the author once heard the folk singer, Odetta, lament):

> Down on me, down on me
> Looks like everybody
> In the whole wide world
> Is down on me

Or picture the release of pain and suffering that occurs when one sings, as B. B. King does in a commercially produced record, of a virtually complete racial history of oppression and misery. He begins his ballad with the slave ship whose crew, carrying whips, stood over large numbers of Blacks. King then bemoans virtually all of the wretchedness of the Black community: rats, roaches, bedbugs, lack of adequate housing, inferior schools, insensitive police, welfare injustices, and so on (King, undated). One famous vocalist has stated that the oppression, pain, and suffering uniquely experienced by Blacks is one necessary precondition for the making of a good blues singer (Blauner, 1972).

Participation in competitive sports is another manifestation of sublimation in the Black adjustment repertoire, especially among Black males (Poussaint, 1970). When superimposed upon a high earning potential and the likelihood of fame, the reason for the overrepresentation of Blacks in professional sports seems to be quite clear. A similar position might be taken regarding Black representation in the performing arts.

Displacement

The turmoil that erupted into violence in many of the larger cities of this nation during the late 1960s and early 1970s was recognized as having been the result of accumulated anger resulting from oppressive conditions (Report of the National Advisory Commission on Civil Disorders, 1968). However, many investigators of these disturbances failed to consider that the behavior of the "rioters" was not a direct lashing out at oppression but rather a *displacement* of responses originally aroused by the oppressor. Rather than attacking "the enemy" directly, the frustrated citizens attacked the symbols of the enemy's presence: appliance stores, clothing stores, apartment buildings, and so forth. Black-owned businesses in these neighborhoods almost never were vandalized.

One of the few Black leaders who articulated an understanding of these dynamics was the late Malcolm X, who, in discussing one such civil disturbance, indicated that rather than being the hoodlums and thieves portrayed by the media, the rioters were frustrated people who were striking out at an unjust system of internal colonialism, victimization, and oppression. The grocery stores, clothing stores, liquor stores, and appliance stores (all of which were owned by people outside of the community) were the closest and most visible symptoms of this injustice and were attacked as a means of unconscious retribution. Because such displacement was an end in itself, the merchandise actually was of little significance, except to verify and validate the effectiveness of the retaliation. In contrast to the view of Malcolm X, this author observed a Black "leader" exclaim on national television that he could not understand why so many Blacks were using the variously precipitating stimuli as "excuses" for theft.

Sexual assault has been used as a means of displacing aggression. Although Cleaver (1968) demonstrated an overawareness of his behavior in this regard, it is doubtful that he was so enlightened prior to his retrospective assessment. Thus, his practice of sexually assaulting White females as vengeance against White males may not have been initially conscious in purpose. Yet, the displacement nature of his behavior is clearly enunciated when he states, "Rape was an insurrectionary act. It delighted me that I was defying and trampling upon the White man's law, upon his system of values, and that I was defiling his women—and this point, I believe, was the most satisfying to me, because I was very resentful over the historical fact of how the White man has used Black women. I felt I was getting revenge" (1968, p. 14). Whether or not consciously determined, such interracial criminal behavior is relatively rare, as we shall see in chapter 7. However, even legitimate socio-sexual behavior between Black males and White females may involve displacement. One investigator of interracial marriages reported that "three of the Black husbands confessed that their initial desire to date interracially may have stemmed from vindictive feelings against White males. In the opinion of these Blacks, the seduction and marriage of a White female defied one of White society's most rigorous taboos" (Porterfield, 1973).

Humor

Another coping mechanism or adjustment technique utilized by Blacks is that of humor, which also evolved from the frustration of slavery. Whether in Oscar Brown's "The Signifying Monkey" or David Carrothers's "An Indignation Dinner," Black humor is replete with tension-relieving tales of accomplishment by means of shrewdness, craftiness, guile, and trickery (Comer, 1972). As Comer points out, "What was verbalized in jest only reflected what frequently was being acted out in the Black and White relationship—beat the system, beat the man; beat the White man who is the system" (1972, p. 177). Much of the structure of this humor seems to be a preservation of the African folk tales, mentioned in chapters 1 and 7, in which more powerful animals often are outwitted ingeniously by less powerful ones. This type of humor actually is a form of identification, where the oppressed vicariously experience the success of the weaker animal.

A Specifically Unique Mechanism

One adjustment technique, prevalent among Blacks but virtually absent among Whites, has been described by Grier and Cobbs as "weeping without feeling" (1968). This symptom involves "a Black man passively viewing another man, Black or White, triumphant over odds and standing supreme in a moment of personal glory" (1968, p. 61). These tears seem to come without warning and appear to be unrelated to any feeling or thought which might cause the subject to feel sad. The explanatory dynamics are related to the unconscious feelings of sadness regarding accomplishments which were denied to the subject.

CHAPTER SEVEN

Personality

> It is impossible to find much of anything that is unique or general in American Negro personality, excepting only an almost, if not quite, ubiquitous fear of white people. (Harry Stack Sullivan, 1940, p. 175)

Definition of Personality

In view of the many themes and circumscriptions regarding personality, it is difficult to present an all-encompassing definition. In 1937, Gordon Allport, after having searched the literature, discovered 50 separate definitions of this concept (cited in Goleman et al., 1982). Also, after a thorough review of theory and research, Hall and Lindzey reported in 1978 that there is no universally accepted definition of personality. However, the definition given by Hinsie and Campbell (1970) seems to encapsulate the basic concepts found in most other definitions. These authors tell us that personality is

> the characteristic, and to some extent predictable, behavior-response patterns that each person evolves, both consciously and unconsciously, as his style of life (1970, p. 556)

Explaining further, these authors state that "the personality represents the compromise between inner drives and needs, and the controls that limit or regulate their expression . . . the personality functions to maintain a stable, reciprocal relationship between the person and his environment . . . the personality, in other words, is a set of habits that characterize the person in his way of managing day-to-day living; under ordinary conditions it is relatively stable and predictable. . . ." (1974, p. 556)

Theories on the causal factors in personality development point to one or more of the following: heredity, physiological conditions, childhood experiences, and/or sociocultural determinants. Most currently recognized theories, however, emphasize either early-life or sociocultural factors.

Black Personality

In discussing the personality of Black people, it should be remembered that virtually all of the popular and widely promulgated theories developed by Western psychologists and psychiatrists were constructed on the basis of observing Caucasian behavior. Because Blacks and Whites generally live in two separate cultures with distinctions in almost every aspect of experience, it is reasonable to expect that none of the currently accepted theories explain the Black personality. Prior to the 1960s, several attempts were made to explain Black behavior from a Western (Eurocentric) personality viewpoint, with results that painted a somber and dismal picture of the Black psyche. Myrdal (1944) indicated that the overall denial of opportunity caused Blacks to hate themselves and to adopt White standards. Echoing this same theme, Bryson and Bardo (1975) quote Von Tress as stating that "the most significant component of the Negro personality is his self-hatred for being a member of a downtrodden group" (p. 8). Additionally, Kardiner and Oversey (1951) reported that Blacks are characterized by self-hatred, repressed and suppressed hostility, a White ego-ideal and confused sexual roles. Crain and Weisman cite the following "personality traits and styles of behavior which are statistically more common among blacks than among whites": (1) high rate of violence and crime; (2) high rates of escapism, including use of drugs and alcohol; (3) excessive apathy and timidity; (4) low learning ability in both academic and job situations; and (5) high levels of interpersonal difficulties, especially in marriage (1972, p. 22).

One of the most persistently negative findings regarding the Black personality related to self-concept or self-esteem. Gordon (cited in Smith et al., 1978) analyzed 83 scientific studies of Black self-concept, conducted from 1939 through 1973, and found that between 1939 and 1963 over 87 percent of the studies reported findings of low self-esteem for Black Americans. However, between 1964 and 1973 less than 50 percent of the studies showed low self-esteem for Blacks. Since the studies using interviews tended to show higher Black self-esteem than those using questionnaires or inventories, it is unclear whether the higher self-esteem subsequent to 1964 was due to an actually increased self-regard on the part of the subjects, or was traceable to a change in the way that later experimenters tended to perceive the subjects. The "Black Is Beautiful" movement of the mid-1960s and early 1970s could have influenced the experimenters as well as the subjects.

Two often-cited researchers who found consistently negative self-concepts among Black children are Clark and Clark, who found that by the age of five the Black child is aware that being Black is a mark of inferiority and that "the child himself must be identified with that which he rejects. This situation apparently introduces a fundamental conflict at the very foundation of the ego structure" (1950, p.63). This study and several of the others cited above recently have been reinterpreted by Black psychologists, who have found the original interpretations to have been either invalid or inaccurate (Azibo, 1984). Hence, there have begun to develop several Africentric theories and theorists of Black personality. These new views represent not only paradigmatic shifts in theoretic orientation but also a virtual insurrection in research focus. Instead of finding Black personality to be charcteristically negative (e.g., low self-esteem, self-hatred, feelings of inferiority, etc.) the new positivists are finding the Black personality to be characterized by rich spirituality, a Black world-view, a commitment to Black causes, and an overall drive to improve Black life (Azibo, 1984). However, these characterisitics have been found to be indigenous to African heritage rather than merely a reaction to racial oppression. It follows, then, that one cannot understand the personality of Africans or their descendants anywhere in the world without a knowledge of the basic sources from which the personality derives. The argument among scholars and researchers regarding the nature and degree of African survivals in the New World includes considerations regarding a wide range of traditions and customs as expressed in music, art, language, childrearing practices, and so on. Though these discussions of cultural transplantations rarely include personality characteristics, it is most probable that the early Africans brought to the Americas culturally unique behavior-response patterns that were deeply imbedded in their beings. Understanding current Black personality, therefore, requires a thorough knowledge of the factors that were instrumental in molding it. Herskovits, reflecting on the survival of traits and characteristics when a minority group is assimilated into a majority group, indicates that in most cases "those traits which survive the longest under cultural contact form the least tangible manifestations of culture" (1935, p. 260). Because of the many covert, subliminal, nonverbal, and otherwise seemingly innocuous means of culturally transmitting and conditioning personality from parent to offspring, it is possible that personality represents the most profound and intense of all African survivals.

One aspect of this personality is the African's interpersonal rather than individualistic orientation towards the world. This outlook perceives all nature as being in a system that is interconnected, interrelated, and incomplete harmony. Furthermore, the system is seen as requiring reciprocal interaction between all elements (Tempels, 1952; Mbiti, 1969; Khoapa, 1980). Thus "philosophy, theology, politics, social theory, land law, medicine, birth, burial—all find themselves concentrated in a system so tight that to exclude one item from the whole is to paralyze the structure as a whole." Amplifying on this point, Tempels (1952) tells us that:

> Just as Bantu Ontology is opposed to the European concept of individuated things, existing in themselves, isolated from others, so Bantu Psychology cannot conceive of man as an individual, as a force existing by itself and apart from its ontological relationships with other living beings and from its connection with the animals or inanimate forces around it. The Bantu cannot be a lone being. It is not a good enough synonym for that to say that he is a social being. No; he feels and knows himself to be a vital force, at this very time to be in intimate and personal relationship with other forces acting above him and below him in the hierarchy of forces. He knows himself to be a vital force, even now influencing some forces and being influenced by others. The human being, apart from the ontological hierarchy and the interaction of forces, has no existence in the conceptions of the Bantu. (Pp. 68–69)

There is an even more intense interrelationship among the living organisms. Man shares biological life with animals but by virtue of his spirituality becomes distinguished from the animals. The institution of marriage, being the uniting link in the rhythm of life, symbolizes and reflects this interrelationship, since it binds together all generations. Past generations extending to the most distant ancestors are represented in one's parents, while all future generations are represented in one's children. It is through one's offspring, then, that one's life is extended, both into the past and into the future. Children, therefore, are most highly esteemed in the life of the African.

Another symptom of the African interconnectionism is the concept of family, or kinship. Mbiti explains that:

> The deep sense of kinship, with all it implies, has been one of the strongest forces in traditional African life. Kinship is reckoned through blood and betrothal (engagement and marriage). It is kinship which controls social relationships between

> people in a given community: It governs marital customs and regulations, it determines the behavior of one individual towards another. Indeed, this sense of kinship binds together the entire life of the tribe, and is even extended to cover animals, plants, and nonliving objects through the totemic system. Almost all the concepts connected with human relationships can be understood and interpreted through the kinship system. This it is which largely governs the behavior, thinking, and whole life of the individual in the society of which he is a member. (P. 104)

Mbiti further describes this kinship system as being like a "vast network" which stretches in every direction to include all of the people in any given local group. This means that everyone is related to everyone else in some way, thereby providing each member of the group with hundreds of uncles, aunts, fathers, mothers, sons, daughters, and other kin. In addition to extending laterally, the kinship system also extends vertically to include those yet to be born and those who have departed this life. To the African, every gathering of people is simply an extension of the family (Khoapa, 1980). Because of this feeling of kinship, it is normal for Africans to simply "drop by" the home of another without a special invitation, simply to engage in conversation. This is in direct contrast to the behavior and expectations of many Westerners. Commenting on this contrast, Mphahlele (cited in Khoapa) states that "I have not yet seen an African explore territory or climb mountains for mere conquest; I have not yet seen him sit on a lonely rock or river bank or lake fishing; . . . I have not yet seen an African go out to lonely places for a vacation, just for the scenery. We go to other people."

We can see, therefore, that the African's sense of interconnectionism has a strong interpersonal component. Focusing on this position, Nobles (1980) tells us that unlike the world-view of Europeans, the Africentric outlook on life is characterized by "cooperation," "interdependence," and "collective responsibility." As a consequence, "interrelatedness, connectedness, and interdependence are viewed as the unifying philosophic concepts in the Afro-American experience base" (Nobles, cited in White, 1984, p. 35).

Even in African moral development, most of the focus is on social conduct rather than on individual behavior (Khoapa, 1980). This emphasis on social conduct, according to Khoapa, is an outgrowth of the African view that the individual exists only because others exist. Hence, moral laws facilitate not only the fulfilling of individual obligations to society, but also the enjoying of certain rights and privileges in society. "Morals are what have produced the virtues that society appreciates and endeavors to preserve, such as friendship, compassion, love, honesty, justice, courage, self-control, etc. On the other hand, morals also sharpen people's dislikes and avoidance of vices like theft, cheating, selfishness, greed, etc." (Khoapa, 1980, p. 11). One can observe this type of moral development in many African-related communities throughout the Caribbean, where among populations almost entirely Black, police are not armed, bus drivers carry their fares in open boxes without fear of robbery, and tourists leave unlocked bicycles and scooters unattended on the street for hours without fear of theft. A further unfolding of this African interconnectionism-interpersonalism is a political structure built around socialism, which is merely an extension of the African family and African society. Hence, African socialism is quite different from Western socialism. Making this distinction, Khoapa (1980) reminds us that African socialism differs from both Marxist socialism and the type of Western socialism that is found in Britain or Sweden. African socialism focuses on universal charity and codes of conduct which have given dignity to people regardless of their station in life. It refers to "the African's thought processes and cosmological ideas which regard man not as a social means but as an end and entity in society" (p. 24). Rather than looking upon one class of men as his brothers and another class as his enemies, the African regards all men as members of his ever-extending family. According to Khoapa, the term "familyhood" comes closest to describing the type of socialism towards which Africans aspire. This difference between Western and African socialism was observed in the study by Greenfield and Bruner (1971) cited in chapter 4. These authors saw African socialism as merely an updating of existing social conditions, whereas Western socialism was viewed as a radical revolution. Also, Greenfield and Bruner were able to provide scientific evidence for the collectivism-interpersonalism on the part of Africans. In their report, several experiments were conducted among the Wolof in Senegal, West Africa. Using Wolof children and intending to study the Piaget's Concept of Conservation, the authors report that:

> Wolof families evaluate and interpret the child's motor activity in terms of the relation of this activity to the people around him. That is, the Wolof child's first steps are not treated as beginning mastery of the walking process, but as evidence of the child's desire to move nearer to another person . . . a social interpretation of an act not only relates the actor

> to the group, but also relates the group—including the actor—to physical events. (P. 74)

Greenfield and Bruner point out additionally that individualistic orientations which would separate the Wolof child from the group are discouraged by the Wolof culture. "Thus, the collective orientation is systematically encouraged as socialization progresses" (p. 74).

Among Western descendants of Africans, this interpersonalism-collectivism may serve as a means of maintaining a general sense of peoplehood. However, such an orientation is incompatible and in constant conflict with a society that is focused on individualism. For example, this author has observed that at most predominantly White universities, faculty members are required to reserve a minimum of three office hours per week for the counseling and advising of students. This minimum, however, traditionally has become also the maximum. Black faculty at these universities, on the other hand, devote considerably more time to working with Black students, serving on committees, arranging and participating in workshops, giving special lectures, and so on, rather than pursuing individual research interests. Correspondingly, Black students tend to expect this type of response and often express a sense of betrayal regarding the behavior of "research-oriented" Black faculty. This author has encountered many Black professionals in academia who admit a feeling of discomfort when they attempt to "save themselves" by producing more research and thereby limiting their interpersonal contacts. Thus, the conflict of values that occurs among Black faculty on White campuses is symptomatic of the disaccord between Africentric interpersonalism and Eurocentric individualism. This clash is exacerbated by tenure and promotion decisions, which usually subordinate those duties and tasks which Black faculty, as a function of their heritage, regard as most important. This overall problem is greatly reduced at predominantly Black colleges where, in accordance with the predisposed interpersonalism and sense of kinship, the main emphasis is on the teaching, counseling, and guidance of students. Accordingly, at many of these institutions the minimum frequency of office hours, officially mandated, is 12 per week.

A further indication of the degree to which this African heritage conflicts with Western values was emphasized by the results of a systematic investigation of Black consumer cooperatives (Williams, 1977). Accessing eight major such cooperatives in the New York City area, Williams found that the familial-interpersonalistic-collectivistic pursuits, with their special sphere of attitudes and behaviors, were incongruous with the orientation and attitudes required for pursuit of monetary profits. Since some profits were necessary for the success of the cooperatives, most of them experienced financial failure.

Another African trait is the belief that wisdom and mental acuteness are superior to strength (Herskovits, 1935). This may come as a surprise to those Westerners who emphasize Black achievement in sports while simultaneously accepting the notion of Black intellectual inferiority. However, this African belief in the superiority of mental acumen is inculcated into the African youth at a very early age, primarily through the telling of the animal stories mentioned earlier. According to the Herskovits document, these animal stories represent the most important factor in imparting moral principles to African youth. These stories, common throughout Black Africa, describe a shrewd animal who outwits his bigger but slower and intellectually less-able opponents, eventually subordinating them completely "In similar manner, the African child is taught that the old are wiser than the young, that malice often brings about destruction, that impetuousness is dangerous, that obedience is rewarded, and other moral precepts of like character" (Herskovits, 1935, p. 228). One African trait which seems to be conspicuously present among Black males throughout the diaspora is the propensity for creativity in verbal expression. This predisposition results from the African's interest in court procedure, which sharpens the verbal facility. On this point we are told that:

> As a result of their interest in court procedure, most African men have a great proficiency in argumentation and in skillful presentation of a case before a judicial body. This argumentation is carried on with a wealth of allusion, characterized by the use of a vivid and often poetic imagery and the employment of many proverbs. The effect of this style of presentation is that it enables the African, in displaying his histrionic ability to make his points much more strikingly and persuasively than a bare presentation of the facts could possibly do. (Herskovits, 1935, p. 230)

Thus, we see a strong possibility that the often-observed "rapping" ability of Blacks, in addition to having been shaped by oral tradition, may have been predisposed by these conditioned experiences of skillful argumentation.

Other personality characteristics of Africans are the reluctance to give a quick answer to a question and the tendency to give the answer his questioner wishes to recieve. Regarding this matter, Herskovits comments that "the phrasing of the Dutch Guiana Bush Negro, who said 'long ago our ancestors taught us that it is unwise for a man to tell anyone more than half of what he knows about anything', would hold significance for any African or New World Negro" (p. 261).

Aggressiveness

Many individuals, in spite of lack of evidence, persistently believe that Blacks are innately more aggressive than Whites (Baughman, 1971). However, in addition to the tendency towards the repression of aggression mentioned in chapter 5, there is some empirical evidence that Blacks may be less aggressive than Whites. For example, one study of an all-Black community in the United States found that it had not had a murder in 20 years (Baughman, 1971). Another study of 41 tribes in East Africa found that they "had lower homocide rates than the whites of either South Carolina or Texas" (Pettigrew, cited in Baughman, 1971). Additionally, Grossack (1957) in a study of 171 Black college males and females, using the Edwards Personal Preference Schedule as the measure of personality, found that there was no statistically significant difference between Black males and White males as far as aggressive needs were concerned. The Black females, though significantly lower in aggression than the Black males, were higher than the White females. Also, Mussen (cited in Grossack, 1963), using the Thematic Apperception Test with 100 Black and White boys at a summer camp, analyzed the strength of five types of aggressive needs: (1) self-defense aggression; (2) physical-social aggression; (3) emotional, verbal aggression; (4) destruction, smashing, breaking; and (5) killing in anger. He discovered that the Blacks, when compared to the whites, perceived the environment as being more hostile. However, killing in anger and self-defense aggression were lower for the Blacks than for the Whites. Blacks were higher than Whites in emotional, verbal aggression and were equal to the Whites in terms of other aggressive needs. Thus, the Black boys tended to see the world as threatening but indulged in more verbal aggression and hostile thinking than in more extreme expressions of aggression. Hence, the high incidence of Black-on-Black crime within the inner cities of our larger metropolitan areas probably is due to the accumulation of unbearable frustration among a restricted category of Blacks, rather than being characteristic of any racially extensive predisposition (see chapter 7).

The widespread belief among Whites that Blacks in general, contrary to evidence, are indigenously hyperaggressive, may be caused by a combination of inappropriate generalizations, logical expectations, and projection (Baughman, 1971). Baughman points out that

Whites observe the magnitude of overt physical aggression in the Black community and not only erroneously ascribe this behavior to all Blacks, but also fail to recognize it as displacement of hostility towards Whites. Moreover, Whites logically conclude that Blacks *should* be angry and aggressive, given the wretched treatment they have received in this country for nearly 400 years. Finally, since some evidence (cited above) has shown Whites to be the more aggressive race, their perception of greater Black aggression might be a White projection, causing them to avoid awareness of their own hostility and aggression by assigning these characteristics to Blacks.

Other Personality Characteristics

Even prior to the thrust of the present-day positivists, some investigators found Blacks to have favorable and beneficial traits in comparison with Whites. For example, Grossack, in the 1963 report of his study with the Edwards Personal Preference Schedule, found Black females to be higher than White females on the need for achievement and no difference between the Black and White males on this variable. Also the Black males and females surpassed the Whites of both sexes in the matter of the need to have things organized, neat, and well-planned. The study also found Black males to be higher than White males in endurance, with no racial difference between the females on this variable. Hence, the data shows the subjects to be the exact opposite of the "lazy, shiftless" stereotype. The results concerning endurance not only may provide further understanding of Black survival in the past, against overwhelming odds, but also could afford hope for the future. The previously reported study by Mussen (cited in Grossack, 1963), using the Thematic Apperception Test with Black and White boys at a summer camp, discovered that there were significantly more Blacks than Whites who were high on "understanding" and significantly fewer Blacks than Whites who were high on feelings of rejection.

It is quite likely that the fledgling Black positivism will produce empirical evidence in support of additionally favorable Black personality traits and characteristics that are based on African spirituality and cosmology. The most widely promulgated theory out of which such scientific illumination has begun to develop is the Africentric Theory of Black Personality formulated by Baldwin (1976, 1981). According to Baldwin, African cosmology, as a function of its focus on the interrelatedness of nature, regards biological and psychological phenomena as being interrelated and interdependent. It also views heredity and environment as being interrelated, with heredity being dominant. Within this cosmological framework, African personality develops; but because of the hereditary dominance, the basic underpinnings of this personality are biogenetic, and a major aspect of its development is an unconcious but innate "self-extension orientation" or "urge for mergence." There also is a push for a complete involvement with experience, resulting in a "spiritualistic transcendence." Also growing out of the self-extension orientation is an African self-consciousness which is "the conscious level process of communal phenomenology" (Baldwin, 1981, p. 174) and thereby involves a strong interpersonalism. Being conscious, this African self-consciousness is subject to social-environmental influences and represents the African survival thrust. The significant point is that all Blacks possess this natural, innate predisposition. It simply is more dominant in some and more suppressed in others, due to early socialization and conditioning.

Baldwin and Bell (1985) have developed a standardized personality questionnaire to evalute this African personality, and significant research interest is being focused on both the questionnaire and the theory upon which it is based.

CHAPTER EIGHT

Socially Deviant and Self-Destructive Behavior

> Blacks who have grown up in the United States have different amounts and different kinds of psychological scar tissue . . . so we have our own unique and private ways of reacting to the slings and arrows of outrageous racism. (Edwards, 1972)

Criminal Behavior

According to *Webster's Third New International Dictionary* (1971), crimes are of two types: felonies and misdemeanors. A felony is a violation of the law for which punishment is death or imprisonment in excess of one year, whereas a misdemeanor is a violation which is not punishable by death or imprisonment in a state penitentiary. Juvenile delinquency is defined by the same dictionary as "behavior by minors of not more than a specific age, usually eighteen years, that is antisocial or in violation of the law" (p. 767). Hence, the distinction between criminality and juvenile delinquency is based on the age of the offender, rather than the nature or severity of the violation. The widespread misconception that juvenile delinquency involves only minor violations of the law possibly stems from the recognition that such delinquency, in most states of the Union, includes not only acts defined under the adult criminal code but also minor acts that are not included within the adult criminal code. These minor acts, such as truancy, running away from home, curfew violation, and so on, being restricted to youth, often are perceived as constituting the essence of juvenile delinquency. The fact that a fourteen-year-old bank robber or forcible rapist legally can be charged with only juvenile delinquency may come as a surprise to most people.

In his discussion of deviance within the Black community, Blackwell

(1985) presents a wealth of demographic information regarding the current status of Black crime. However, he cautions that statistics on crime, particularly with regard to incidence, generally are inaccurate. One reason for this is that there is a lack of interjurisdictional uniformity in reporting crime. Another factor is that some crimes are not reported to the authorities, and a third factor is the differential perception on the part of law enforcement officials as to what sorts of activities constitute criminal behavior. Blackwell identifies this latter factor as a major reason for the disproportionate representation of Blacks among criminal offenders. In comparison with Whites, Blacks are more often arrested (four times more frequently than Whites), more often brought to trial, more often sentenced, and less often paroled. Another cause of the overrepresentation of Blacks in the criminal statistics is that the Black population is considerably younger than the White population. Hence, disproportionately more Blacks are in the high-crime age groups, thereby inflating the Black crime rate. Still another factor underlying the disproportionately high arrest rates among Blacks is the "demographic bias" exhibited by some police departments. This type of bias is occasioned by the observation that:

> Police officers may be more likely to patrol those ecological areas of a community that are characterized by a high rate of crime, and if police officers enter those areas with a high expectation of discovering criminal activity, then they are more likely to find criminal behavior in actions they might be more inclined to dismiss if observed in other areas of the metropolitan community. Blacks complain, justifiably so, that they are subjected to unwarranted stopping, questioning, searching, and arresting when there is no evidence that a crime has been committed. (Blackwell, 1985, p. 303)

Wth the above limitations taken into account, Blackwell presents the following picture of Black felonies as of 1979, with Blacks accounting for 11 percent of the total population: Of all persons arrested for murder and nonnegligent manslaughter in the United States, 47.7 percent were Black, and in urban areas, the rate was 54.7 percent. In the United States, Blacks accounted for 37 percent of aggravated assault arrests, 47.7 percent of forcible rape arrests, more than 50 percent of robbery arrests, and 28.7 percent of burglary arrests. In addition, 47 percent of all prison inmates were Black.

Blacks are disproportionately represented not only among the offenders but also among the victims of violent crime. Murder is the fourth overall cause of death among Blacks, and the leading cause of death among male Blacks between the ages of 20 and 29. Interestingly, this age range greatly overlaps the age range for heightened suicide among Black males. Black male homicide victims more than doubled between 1960 and 1979, and Black female victims increased by 80 percent. In addition, Black and other minority women have a rape victimization rate that is almost double that of White women (Blackwell, 1985).

A 1973 article in *Newsweek* magazine indicated that in the city of Detroit, most of the murders take place in the Black community. In 1972, there were 690 murder victims city-wide, and 575 of them were Black. In addition, 590 of the killers were Black. Even allowing for false, biased, and/or otherwise misleading statistics, this represents a staggering amount of Black-on-Black violence. Some have suggested that this violence is caused by substance abuse, especially alcohol, but the research tends to be unclear regarding such a connection. Lewis et al. (1983), in an investigation with 237 Whites and 72 Blacks, all adults, found that the Whites showed a higher relationship between antisocial behavior and alcoholism than did the Blacks. On the other hand, Dawkins and Dawkins (1983), in a study with 340 juvenile delinquents, reported the relationship between drinking and antisocial offenses to be greatest for Blacks, with Whites and Hispanics in second and third places respectively.

Most investigators, however, trace the problem to pent-up aggression caused by the frustration of being Black in White America. Thus, Blacks kill other Blacks because experience has taught that such expression of aggression is safe as well as condoned, and that directly confronting Whites can be extremely dangerous. Commenting on this point, Poussaint explains that:

> All too frequently are black crimes against blacks dismissed as unworthy of the white man's lofty attention. White law enforcers were not greatly concerned with drug addiction until it spread beyond the ghettoes to the suburbs. . . .
>
> Commonly, when blacks hurt blacks, they are given a light sentence or released. Many white officials countenance flagrant police corruption in the ghetto and disregard black violence since, after all, "It's only niggers cutting each other up". The lack of worth attributed to a black man's life becomes particularly noticeable when judged against the high premium placed on the white man's life. In fact, it seems too often as if the function of the police is to protect whites from blacks, thereby restricting law enforcement to the area beyond the ghetto.

> If a black man rapes a white woman, he may get the electric chair. However, when a white man murders a black man or rapes a black woman, he is let off lightly, particularly if he is a policeman. The crime figures show that fewer whites are killed by blacks than the reverse, which would seem to indicate the black man's awareness that if he "messes" with "whitey", he will really get into trouble. . . .
>
> Thus, it becomes safe in the minds of many blacks to abuse their own people, while they remain internally fearful of confronting the white man. (1972, pp. 73–74)

Indeed, it has been this danger of affronting Whites that for centuries has caused the severe repression of aggressive tendencies in Black males within the United Sates (Grier & Cobbs, 970). The current manifestations of Black-on-Black violence, then may represent unconsciously motivated expression of escalating pressure which, as a cumulative effect, no longer can be contained and which is displaced onto a safe substitute. Such behavior is similar to that of the husband who beats his wife and children rather than confront the overbearing and punitive boss; or the child who, instead of opposing his parent or teacher, instigates a fight with a weaker youngster. That this behavior is not motivated at the level of conscious awareness does not render it any less deleterious. However, the cure for such problem behavior necessitates more than simply recognizing the underlying cause. In the case of Black-on-Black violence, we cannot afford only to be aware that much of the cause is traceable to White oppression. Such recognition, however insightful, will not in itself culminate in resolution. As indicated by Poussaint (1972), Black communities must not be passive about Blacks abusing other Blacks and should devise programs of community self-help. Such programs should be planned not only to prevent wayward behavior but also to rehabilitate any transgressors. Central to such planning is a need to intervene positively in the early years of the developing child's life and to gain greater community control over the judicial system.

Substance Abuse

According to the latest manual of the American Psychiatric Association (DSM-III), agents of substance use are alcohol, barbituates, amphetamines, opioids, cocaine, phencyclidine (PCP), hallucinogens, cannabis (marijuana), and tobacco. A pattern of pathological use of any of these agents constitutes a substance use disorder. Because alcoholism is the most widespread health problem in America, except for cancer and heart disease, it has been studied more extensively than any other substance use disorder. Alcoholism has been defined as:

> A chronic disorder manifested by undue preoccupation with alcohol to the detriment of physical and mental health; a loss of control when drinking has begun, although it may not be carried to the point of intoxication; and a self-destructive attitude in dealing with relationships and life situations. (Chafetz, cited in Brodie, 1973, p. 8)

However, there is surprisingly little known about the actual incidence or physical and psychological effects of this disorder. On the matter of effects, Brodie (1973) points out that of all the drugs reviewed and reported upon by the National Council on Marijuana and Drug Abuse, alcohol has the widest use and the longest history. He also points out that in our society 77 percent of all men and 60 percent of all women drink at least once per year, and public intoxication accounts for one-third of all arrests reported annually. Yet, the scientific information regarding the effects of alcohol is no greater than that for other drugs discovered more recently and used by a small fraction of the 95 million Americans who annually consume alcohol (Brodie, 1973). With regard to Blacks, there is an even more profound absence of information. "Social scientists know less about alcoholism, excessive drinking, or social drinking among Blacks than perhaps any other racial or ethnic group in America" (Blackwell, 1985, p. 33). In a massive 1,242-page report, the National Commission on Marijuana and Drug Abuse (1973) devoted a full chapter to substance abuse among Native Americans and virtually no information regarding Blacks. However, the report does indicate that Blacks, Irish Catholics, Latin Americans, and Caribbeans show the highest rate of social consequence drinking. Although it may be reasonable to conclude that among Blacks the effects of alcohol would be essentially the same as among Whites, there is a dearth of information here, and data regarding cross-cultural incidence, prevalence, etiology, and treatment are difficult to find. What information is available consistently shows that alcoholism among Blacks is disproportionately high. However, information concerning the other substances, as far as Blacks are concerned, is extremely sparse (Smith et al., 1978).

The effects of alcohol are a function of the individual's personality, past drug experience, physiological status, rate of absorption, and rate of excretion. However, the most important factor is the Blood

Alcohol Concentration (Brodie, 1973). This Blood Alcohol Concentration (BAC) results not only from the amount of alcohol consumed but also from the individual's degree of tolerance, the rate of metabolism, and the rate of absorption from the gastrointestinal tract. With increased levels of BAC, there are negative effects on all sense modalities and sensorimotor performance. A single large dose has been found to cause reduction in rapid eye movement (REM) during sleep and an increase in various sympathetic nervous system responses. Also, there is impairment of verbal fluency, learning ability, memory, intellectual functions, time perception, and general motivation. Increased risk-taking also is a much observed effect. The only beneficial consequences of alcohol intake are the stimulation of appetite and the calming or tranquilizing effect (Brodie, 1973).

With regard to Blacks, most of the studies on substance abuse focus on alcohol alone, and even here the data usually are restricted to demographics, rates, incidence, and prevalence, rather than dealing with racially differential causal factors. The overall consensus among these studies is that alcohol use is greater among Whites than among Blacks, and also greater among males than among females. For example, Morgan et al. (1985), in a study at the San Diego Job Corps Center, involving 111 Hispanics, 69 Indo-Chinese, 67 Whites, and 67 Blacks, discovered that 85 percent were drinking one to five times per week and 14 percent were having weekend "binges" of more than 20 drinks. Caucasians began drinking at an earlier age than did the other groups, and 60 percent of the total sample reported medical, legal, or vocational problems resulting from drinking. Caetano (1984) evaluated the drinking patterns and alcohol-related problems of 1,206 Blacks (468 males and 738 females), 2,327 Whites (1,047 males and 1,280 females), and 634 Hispanics (279 males and 355 females). He discovered that, for Whites, alcohol-related problems decreased between the 18–29- and 20–29-year-old age groups; for Blacks, the problems increased between these two age groups. He discovered also that although the nonwhites had more liberal attitudes toward alcohol use than did the Whites, Black and Hispanic females had higher rates of abstention than White females. The males, however, were similar across ethnic groups. This lower alcohol use by Black females as compared with White females, as well as the lack of distinction between Black and White males, was corroborated by Humphrey et al. (1983), in a sample of 1,044 undergraduates. These investigators found that alcohol intoxication was greater for the males than for the females. Klatsky et al., (1983), accessing 5,976 persons who had routine health examinations at a California medical care program between 1978 and 1980, discovered that drinking behavior was reported by 89.5 percent of the Whites, 84.8 percent of the Latins, 81.9 percent of the Japanese, 79 percent of the Blacks, 68.1 percent of the Chinese, and 63.9 percent of the Filipinos. Again, men of all races reported more drinking than did the women.

Less distinct than the racial/ethnic differences in the incidences of alcohol abuse are the differential *causes* of this problem. Although alcoholism is the most widely studied substance-abuse problem, few researchers have investigated the differential etiology of Black alcohol abuse. Many investigators explain the problem in terms of general theories of alcoholism, such as social conditioning, genetic biology, family psychopathology, and specific personality characteristics (Smith et al., 1978). One investigator (Catanzaro, cited in Smith et al., 1978) concluded from several studies that, rather than being inherited, alcoholism is related to the psychopathology of the alcoholic's family environment. The unhealthy environment is charcterized by sex-role confusion, guilt, compulsiveness, overdependency, anger, anxiety in interpersonal relationships, inability to express emotions adequately, perfectionism, feelings of isolation, emotional immaturity, ambivalence towards authority, low self-esteem, grandiosity, and low tolerance for frustration. Those who address Black alcoholism differentially tend to agree that it is traceable to underutilization of health-care facilities and is also caused by the individual's attempts to escape from racism, poverty, exploitation, and denial of equal opportunities (Larkins, cited in Smith et al., 1978; Watts & Wright, 1984). On this point, Jacobs (cited in Smith et al., 1978) found that in a random sample of Blacks, Chicanos, and Whites taken from the Los Angeles General Hospital, 75 percent were unemployed and 45 percent were between the ages of 20 and 39, which is also, for Blacks, the approximate age for maximum suicide and homicide, neither of which are related to any genetic underpinnings, and both of which are "allied" to environmental stresses. The possibility that Black alcoholism as compared with White alcoholism may not be due to differential personality factors also was suggested by the research of Walters (1983). Comparing male alcoholics (27 Blacks and 27 Whites) with nonalcoholics (46 Blacks and 46 Whites) and using the MacAndrew Alcoholism Scale of the MMPI, Walters found that for Whites there was a significant difference between the alcoholics and nonalcoholics. For Blacks, there was no such difference. However, there was a significant difference between Black and White *nonalcoholics,* with the Blacks being higher. These data seem to suggest that the same tensions and stresses relating to alcohol abuse among White males are present in *all* Black males.

However, only some Blacks seek relief in alcoholism. The reason for this state of affairs would seem to pose an interesting subject for further research.

Alcohol abuse also is related to suicide, although the relationship is not clear. Brodie's 1973 document reports Menninger's belief that alcoholism, is a midway point between social problems and suicide, and that alcoholism, actually represents a partial suicide. This view, according to Brodie, was and is shared by several others, including R. W. Maris, E. G. Palola, B. Rush, and W. A. Rushing. Also, in a comparison of the suicides of alcoholics with those of depressed nonalcoholics, Murphy and Robbins (cited in Solomon & Arnon, 1979) found that at the time of suicide fewer of the alcoholics were married, a significantly higher percentage of the married alcoholics were divorced, and half of the married alcoholics were separated at the time of their suicide. In addition, half of the alcoholics were living alone when they committed suicide. Most interestingly, 48 percent of the alcoholics, as compared with 15 percent of the depressed nonalcoholics, had experienced the loss of a major social relationship within the year prior to the suicide, and two-thirds of these losses occurred six weeks prior to the suicide.

The available information on the use of substances other than alcohol among Blacks is extremely sparse. The 1983 data of Humphrey et al. indicated that there was no difference between Black and White males in marijuana use. However, there was higher use by Black females than by White females, and overall greater use by males than by females. The study by Gary and Berry (1984) indicates that attitudes towards substance use in the Black community depend upon a variety of factors. Using 411 Black males and females as subjects in a stratified random sample, these authors found that those who had least tolerant attitudes towards the use of substances were women, persons over age 64, married persons, those active in the church, those involved in the community, and those who were more racially conscious. That no single personality pattern characterizes Black male heroin addicts and that heroin use does not necessarily lead to heroin addiction among Blacks was reported in a study by Crawford et al. (1983). Crawford's finding of no distinctive pattern among Black addicts conflicts with the characteristics of addicts in general as presented by Stephens (cited in Smith et al., 1978). Stephens describes the addict, unlike the nonaddict, as showing "cool-cat behavior," "conning" behavior, and antisocial behavior. Since it is likely that all Blacks, especially in the inner city, show the above-mentioned behavior in order to survive in a system that is stacked against them, the lack of any distinctive pattern among the addicts in the Crawford study is not surprising and italicizes the probability that general theories of addiction and other troublesome behavior may not be applicable to the Black community.

Suicide

The first known document dealing with suicide is an Egyptian record written between 2000 and 1900 B.C., and the earliest suicide mentioned in Greek literature is that of Jocasta, mother of Oedipus (Hatton et al., 1977). The attitudes of the ancient Greeks and Romans towards suicide varied widely between condemnation and admiration, between approval and strong disapproval of suicide as a means of escaping suffering. For example, Pythagoras, the Greek philosopher, believed that as soldiers of God, humans had no right to leave this world without God's permission. Yet, both Socrates and Aristotle committed suicide (Hatton et al., 1977). Although the taking of one's own life was condemned by the early Judaic, Christian, and Islamic religions, neither the testaments nor the Koran spelled out a prohibition against suicide per se. Rather, the general taboos against the spilling of man's blood, such as are found in the ninth chapter of Genesis, were thought to apply also to the spilling of one's own blood (Hankoff & Einsidler, 1979).

More recent attitudes towards suicide in various cultures range from glorification, through acceptance, to condemnation. The Eskimos and the Hopi Indians of Arizona, for example, do not consider suicide to be morally unacceptable (Brandt, 1954), and some Japanese, especially those of the Samurai tradition, consider hara-kiri (voluntary self-destruction) to be honorable (Chamberlain 1927). That aspects of these cross-culturally dissimilar attitudes towards self-termination are currently present in United States subcultures was demonstrated by Reynolds et al. (1975). These researchers used a sample of 434 subjects, divided equally among Black Americans, Japanese Americans, Mexican Americans, and Euro-Americans (Caucasians). They found that 40 percent of the Blacks and 35 percent of the Mexicans believed that people who commit suicide are either "crazy" or otherwise mentally ill, while only 25 percent of the Whites and 16 percent of the Japanese felt this way. By contrast, 40 percent of the Whites but only 28 percent of the Blacks believed that the suicidal individual is driven by guilt or frustration. Most tellingly, 89 percent of the Blacks believed that suicide is more common among Caucasians than among other races. This belief was true for 68 percent of the Mexicans but only 43 percent of the Whites and 34 percent of the Japanese.

In discussing Black suicide, it is important to recognize that such a phenomenon is abnormal not only from a legal and statistical standpoint, but also from the historical, philosophical, and religious orientations of Black people. Parrinder (1969) informs us that Africans traditionally believe that all death is unnatural, since initially it did not exist among humans. Frequently it is blamed on witches and sorcerers. More often it is viewed as being due to the fault of another creature, usually an animal. The Kono of Sierre Leone believe that God first told humans that they would not die because he would send them new skins. The skins were sent by a dog who stopped along the way and told other animals what he was carrying. The snake overheard, stole the bundle, and changed his skin. Thus the snake does not die, but men die and try to kill snakes. The Lamba of Zambia say that the first man on the earth asked God for some seeds, which were sent in small bundles, one of which was not to be opened. He disobediently opened the forbidden bundle, and death jumped out. The Illa of Zambia say that God offered the first man and woman on earth two bags, one containing life and the other containing death. They chose the shiny bag, which was the wrong one, and death came out (Parrinder, 1969). Thus the Africans believe that death is due to some external causation, and the slaying of oneself is regarded by the African as extremely deviant behavior (Burke, 1974). Usually, the phenomenon is perceived as being caused by witchcraft or insanity, and often the home of the victim is believed to be haunted (Kiev, 1979), The similarity between this African view of the suicidal individual's mental state and the Black American view (mental illness) are worthy of note and again suggest the presence of intangible, less concrete, and more psychological "African survivals."

Because of the Black taboos regarding self-destruction, one logically would expect lower suicide rates for Blacks as compared with Whites, and demographic data show this to be true when Blacks and Whites are compared as composite groups. One finds that most suicides are committed by White males and least by Black females, with Black males and white females in second and third positions respectively (U.S. Bur. of Census, 1978). When the races are compared *as a whole,* the Black suicide rate is half of the White rate (Breed, 1970). For all subcultures and all groups, widowers, widows, and the divorced have higher rates of suicide than do those who are married (Kiev,

1979). In the United States suicide occurs among males more than among females, among Whites more than among Blacks, and among Protestants more than among those of other religions. It also occurs more frequently among those who are downwardly mobile and who have suffered a severe interpersonal loss (Reynolds et al., 1975). It must be observed, however, that accurate data on suicide demographics are difficult to obtain for several reasons. Often the method of death (as opposed to the cause of death) is not known and the officially recorded method may be based on circumstantial evidence which could point inaccurately toward or away from suicide. Thus, recorded accidental deaths and even some homicides might be incorrectly recorded as suicides and vice versa. Also, many newspapers as well as police and other officials acquiesce to the wishes of the victim's relatives, who, because of perceived stigma, implore that the death not be recorded as a suicide. Moreover, public data on Black suicide is even less reliable than data on suicide in general, because of two major factors: the investigative standards of officials are minimal in comparison with more uniform evaluation and documentation regarding White suicide, and the perceived social worth of the individual may influence the recording of suicide data (Peck, 1983). However, as indicated by Hendin (1969), the *overall* suicide rate is confounded by the fact that beginning with age 45, progressively more Whites than Blacks take their own lives. Moreover, elderly Blacks rarely commit suicide, whereas elderly Whites do so at an alarming rate. Of concern to many is the discovery that Black females, though consistently lowest in suicide rate, have shown a 90 percent increase during the past ten years and rapidly are closing in on White females (Breed, 1970; Hauze, 1977).

Although Blacks generally end their own lives less frequently than do Whites, the study by Hendin demonstrates that between the ages of 20 and 35, the suicide rate for Blacks of both sexes is higher than that of Whites for the same age range. His data were taken from the New York City Bureau of Vital Statistics reports, which showed this higher Black rate to be valid for every year between 1921 and 1969. More recent data show the trend to be continuing (Hauze, 1977). Although the overall rates for Blacks in the South have been lower than for those in the North, the Southerners are approaching parity rapidly. However, the Black-White discrepancy within the 20–35 age range does not hold true for the South.

It has been found that the proliferated Black rate at the relatively early ages is traceable to the frustration and anger occasioned by the wretchedness of life for Blacks, particularly in the inner cities of the North. Assessing 25 black suicide attemptors at Harlem, St. Lukes, and Bellevue Hospitals in New York City, Hendin (1969) discovered the subjects to be characterized by uncontrollable rage, homicidal fantasies, self-hatred, and a poor self image. All of these factors become exacerbated by a precipitating factor, such as being fired from a job or being rejected by a member of the opposite sex. Here, it is interesting again to note the possible connection between this extremely deviant behavior and the loss of interpersonalism.

Significantly, the greatly overwhelming increase in suicides by Black females has been found to be related to the loneliness caused by the undersupply of Black males with whom these females can associate (Hauze, 1977). For Black males, the increased incidence between ages 20 and 35 would be even higher if cases of victim-precipitated homicide were included (Seiden, 1970). Victim-precipitated homicide, according to Wolfgang (cited in Hendin, 1970), is homicide in which the victim behaves in a manner that causes another person to kill him. Thus it actually is suicide disguised as homicide. Not infrequently this behavior results from confrontations with police and seems to be caused by despair and rage associated with the injustices and other frustrations of Black urban life. The study by Breed (1970) pointed out that the suicidal Black males in his study, in contrast with the non-suicidal control group, " . . . were much more frequently living alone, and were more likely never married, separated, or living in common-law arrangements" (p. 156). In an earlier essay, Breed points out that *all* suicide is characterized by the loss or absence of something that is desired, and other scholars have defined the "something" as significant interpersonal relationships (Reynolds et al., 1975). Of interest on this point is a relatively recent cross-sectionally comparative study of suicide in primitive societies (Smith & Hackathorn, 1982). These researchers found that suicide was less frequent in societies possessing greater family and political integration, and it was consistently more frequent in societies which emphasized individual pride and shame. One investigator in the United States found, in a population of attempted and completed suicides among White children, that the major difference between the two groups was the presence, in the case of the failed attemptor, of some close friend in whom the child could share confidences (Jan Tausch, 1963). Several other investigators have had similar findings of social isolation and friendlessness among White suicide victims. In one such study, an adolescent victim had been dead in his college dormitory room for 18 days before he was discovered (Seiden, 1966). The fact that on a campus of more than 25,000 students, no one knew or cared enough about the student to question his whereabouts seems to underscore the significance of the interpersonal dimension. If the absence or loss of interpersonalism is such a crucial factor in the suicide of Whites, in spite of their more individualistic orientation, such a loss would seem to be especially crucial in the suicidal behavior of Blacks, whose greater predisposition towards and need for interpersonalism already has been demonstrated. Since there is a relationship among depression, social isolation, and suicide (Durkheim, 1951; Pokorny, 1964), the discussion in chapter 8 of depression and loneliness becomes most relevant. In this regard, Murphy et al. (cited in Beck, 1974), reporting on an international survey of psychiatrists, found that there was an inverse relationship between the frequency of depression and the cohesiveness of the community, thereby underscoring the interpersonalism-individualism variables. In addition, depressive disorder was nonexistent on the African continent until the 1950s, when suicide also began to increase there. Kiev (1979) tells us that the coming of technology to Africa, along with other symptoms of modernization, have caused changes in lifestyles. The major change from tribal to urban living caused a breakdown in family ties and increased isolation. Thus, the African experienced an alienation from tribal beliefs and practices; and this loss of support, along with the decreased interpersonalism, has resulted in increased stress and enhanced potential for suicide. Interestingly, the most vulnerable groups in Africa are the educated and professional classes (Kiev, 1979). Yet, as Kiev points out:

> The frequency of suicide among Africans under urban and Western influences is still very much less than in European society. The traditional or rural African population is still relatively free of either suicide or attempted suicide. Despite problems which no human escapes, these rural Africans possess a social and religious way of life which reduces their risk of suicide by providing individuals with group acceptance and support, and a method of discharging tension. (P. 217)

This persistent and consistent finding of the influence of interpersonalism in the overall mental health of Africans could give some clues as to the possible reduction in, treatment of, and even prevention of suicidal behavior among Blacks in the United States and throughout the African diaspora.

One theory of Black suicide which has not received much attention but which could suggest a progression from environmental frustration to suicide, is the concept of fatalistic suicide. This concept, first suggested by Durkheim (cited in Breed, 1970) argues that some suicides derive from excessive regulation and oppressive discipline and are characterized by the absence of freedom from unjust and arbitrary authorities. These fatalistic suicides have been seen among slaves, prisoners of war, victims of medieval persecution, domestically imprisoned housewives, and excessively regulated adolescents (Breed, 1970). Thus, Breed concludes, the inferior, segregated, powerless position of Blacks in American society renders them to be prime candidates for fatalistic suicide. It is possible, however, that with sufficient interpersonal support, such as provided by a spouse, a close friend, extended family, and so on, the adversity could be endured and possibly even surmounted.

CHAPTER NINE
Mental Disorders

> "Whether by nature or nurture, the personality structure of the Black American is hopelessly abnormal by White American standards." (Thomas & Sillen, cited in Maultsby, 1982)

According to the Psychiatric Dictionary by Hinsie and Campbell, a psychically normal individual "is one who is in harmony with himself and with his environment. He conforms with the cultural requirements or injunctions of his community" (1974, pp. 513–514). For a definition of mental disorder, these authors refer the reader to the latest edition of the *Diagnostic and Statistical Manual of Mental Disorders,* published by the American Psychiatric Association. Goleman (1982) defines abnormal behavior (mental disorder) as that behavior "which is *maladaptive,* that is, it causes personal discomfort and/or violates standards of socially accepted behavior." (p. 417). However, the determination of whether an individual conforms with the requirements of his community or is in harmony with himself and his environment is an inference drawn after evaluating, assessing, and interpreting samples of the subject's verbal and/or nonverbal behavior and relating this behavior to appropriate standards. Yet, the standards almost invariably are based on White, middle-class norms that inappropriately are applied to Blacks by mental health workers who usually have little or no understanding of the Black community's cultural requirements (Baughman, 1971).

Definition of Abnormality

The criterion for diagnosing mental illness in the United States is the *Diagnostic and Statistical Manual* of the American Psychiatric Association. This manual lists every known mental disorder, by title and numerical code, and describes their symptoms. The first manual, published in 1952, listed 60 disorders; the second version (DSM-II) was published in 1968 and listed 145 disorders, while the 1980 edition (DSM-III) describes a total of 230 disorders (Janda & Klenke-Hamel 1982). One criticism of this latter edition is that it includes behaviors which represent only minor problems and should not be listed as psychiatric diagnoses. For example, "drinking too much coffee, being overly shy, academic underachievement, and reading disorders are all included as psychiatric diagnoses. Any of these categories would mean that millions of people who have what most people would consider a minor problem could be given a psychiatric label. This is particularly objectionable to some critics in the case of reading disabilities, because it might stigmatize children so labeled for the rest of their lives" (Goleman et al., 1982, pp. 419–420). The situation is especially disagreeable to Blacks, who view its relevance as extending well beyond reading disabilities. Thus, similar to the dilemma regarding the I.Q., Blacks in the United States find their behavior being judged against inappropriate standards and values, with any differences being interpreted as Black psychopathology. This misdiagnosing of Blacks, as Thomas and Sillen point out (1972), has a long history in the profession of psychiatry. For example, slaves who repeatedly attempted to escape from the "good life" provided by their masters were seen as suffering from "drapetomania," or the "flight from home madness." Those who avoided work or destroyed their masters' property were labeled with the disorder of "dysaethesia aethioptica" (Thomas & Sillen, 1972). These authors also gave evidence of the misrepresentations and actual falsifications of the incidence and prevalence of Black psychosis as presented in the 1840 United States Census. Although deliberate fraud by census officials would be unlikely today, the tendency, based on ignorance or racism, to interpret and label Black behavior incorrectly still persists. For example, there is a persistent belief that Blacks show more psychosis than do Whites (Malzberg, cited in Baughman 1971). On this point, Pasamanick (1963) tells us that ". . . clinicians have stated that because of the inability of White psychiatrists to comprehend the nuances in the Negro subculture, there is the tendency to over-diagnose psychoses among Negroes" (p. 155). This often-cited higher rate of psychosis among Blacks was found by one author to be due to social class rather than to race (Hunt, 1947). His explanation serves to underscore the subtle way in which biased attitudes can intrude into scientific interpretations of racial differences in mental health. Observing that Blacks generally had a higher incidence of psychoses and lower incidence of psychoneuroses, as compared with Whites, and that Blacks higher in social class were similar to Whites in the incidence of these two disorders, Hunt concluded that:

> It may well be that the culturally backward individual is permitted an immediate, primitive, uncritical, emotional expression that is denied the more highly cultural individuals surrounded as he is by limitless social taboos and personal inhibitions. With increasing cultural level, and the individual is deprived of the more immediate and primitive types of emotional expression with the resulting necessity for his conflicts to express themselves through the devious and complicated mechanisms of the psychoneuroses. (P. 136)

Then, subordinating the social class factor and emphasizing the racial variable, Hunt states:

> At present we must limit our conclusions to the statement that psychoneurosis seems relatively less among the Negro mental disorders than among the White, and that the phenomenon is possibly culturally determined. (PP. 135–136)

More recently, Malzberg (cited in Baughman, 1971) reported a 2-to-1 Black-White ratio for schizophrenia, and Wright et al. (1984) reported that among Blacks there has been an overdiagnosis of schizophrenia and an underdiagnosis of life stress, affective disorders, and anxiety disorders. The latter three categories were included among the psychoneuroses prior to the latest edition of the *American Psychiatric Association's Diagnostic and Statistical Manual*. Thus, the belief in high psychosis and low psychoneurosis among Blacks enjoys a persistent preserveration. Wright et al. (1984) point out also that many studies on the diagnosis of Black mental health are biased because of poor data collection, the differential access to and utilization of mental health services by Blacks and Whites, and the difficulty of interpreting much of the data because of client-therapist differences in ethnic background and communication style. Such factors as these, rather than any actually differential preponderance, may account for the reported Black-White discrepancies in the incidence of many mental disorders.

The influence of client-therapist differences on diagnosis was investigated by Baskin et al. (1981). Using Black and White psychiatrists as diagnosticians, these researchers investigated the diagnoses of 1,968 outpatients (Blacks, Whites, Orientals, and Hispanics) who were admitted to the Community Mental Health Center of the Bronx-Lebanon Hospital in New York City during 1979 and 1980. The results indicated that Blacks showed a higher proportion of alcoholism and schizophrenic diagnoses than did any other group. When the diagnoses were assessed in terms of the ethnicity of both the patient and the psychiatrist, it was discovered that the high diagnosis of schizophrenia for Blacks was a function of the perception of White psychiatrists rather than Black psychiatrists. In fact, the Black psychiatrists, who were assigned a total of 271 patients (141 Black and 130 nonblack), diagnosed only two patients (both nonblack) as schizophrenic, while White psychiatrists perceived 15 percent of their total case load and 20 percent of the Blacks as schizophrenic. On the other hand, the Black psychiatrists diagnosed 57 percent of all their patients and 73 percent of the Blacks as being alcoholic. The White psychiatrists gave the alcoholic diagnosis to only 6 percent of all patients and 8 percent of Blacks.

The authors concluded that diagnosis, rather than being an objective assessment, actually is an evaluation of observable behavior compared to the cultural standards of the diagnostician. They further cautioned that some subgroups have life-styles which deviate from that of the general population and that some behavior may be normal in a particular subculture, even though it is considered to be abnormal in another. Such factors as a willingness to challenge the conditions of racism, an awareness of societal hostility towards Blacks, a strong identity with one's own culture, and a need to control one's own destiny have been found to be indicators of positive mental health among Blacks (Wilcox, cited in Smith et al., 1978; Thomas & Comer, 1973). These characteristics indicate responses and adjustments to a possibly hostile society but could be perceived negatively by a diagnostician who is unfamiliar with the Black norm.

Abnormality and Black Behavior

There are few studies which assess the dynamics of mental illness among Blacks, but the investigation by Parker and Kleiner (cited in Bagley, 1968) seems to provide some understanding, much of which verifies the position taken by Wilcox and by Thomas and Sillen, cited above. Using Black interviewers, a heavily Black section of Philadelphia, Pennsylvania was canvassed randomly for Black subjects who subsequently were given a mental health assessment. On the basis of this assessment, the subjects were assigned to either a mentally ill group or a mentally healthy group. To the mentally ill group were added additional Blacks obtained from clinics, hospitals, and psychiatrists. This procedure resulted in 1,423 subjects in the mentally ill group and 1,489 in the mentally healthy sample, all of whom were given a questionnaire designed to measure attitudes on goal-striving (levels of aspiration). The results showed that the mentally ill group set higher goals for themselves than did the mentally healthy group. Furthermore, the mentally ill group denied that being Black constituted any barrier to achievement. In addition, the mentally ill had lower self-esteem and, significantly, the highest incidence of mental illness was discovered in those who were upwardly mobile. Psychotics showed more goal-striving than did neurotics, men showed more mental illness than did women, and younger men revealed more illness than did the older. Commenting on these results, the authors state that: "Despite the relatively closed nature of the opportunity structure for the Negro in American Society, the patients were more prone than the community respondents to perceive the system as open. Along with this perception, they rigidly maintained high levels of goal-striving stress. The existing disjunction involved high levels of goal-striving orientation in the context of an objectively limited opportunity structure" (Bagley, 1968, p. 346).

In addition to the concerns relating to identification and classification are matters regarding the *severity* of the patient's problems. One investigator compared the severity of the symptoms reported by the client with the severity reported by the therapist (Evans, 1984). With Whites as diagnosticians and Blacks, Hispanics, and Whites as subjects, he found that the relationship was strongest for Whites and next for Hispanics, but that there was no relationship for Blacks. Hence, the unresolved cultural relativity problem influences both the range and depth of Black patient assessment. Since proper treatment is based on correct diagnosis, much of the failure in psychotherapeutic intervention with Blacks may be related to these problems of diagnosis.

In contrast with the tendency towards overdiagnosis of Black behavior is the proclivity towards underdiagnosis, especially regarding children in the public schools. Some of the dynamics of this problem were indicted in an investigation by Shechtman (1971). Using a sample of 40 Black children aged 5 to 14, 20 of whom had been referred to a mental health clinic and 20 others of whom were functioning normally, Shechtman found that 60 percent of the clinic patients were referred because of aggressive behavior. She also found that in a 91-item checklist of psychiatric problems, only three items differentiated the clinic patients from the normals: (1) disobedient, rebellious; (2) fighting, assault, and aggressive behavior; and (3) poor schoolwork. Ironically, both the clinic patients and the "normal" students showed the same amount of excessive talking, demanding attention, headaches, nailbiting, stomachaches, and worrying. By contrast, it was found that a sample of White children at the same mental health clinic were referred for stuttering, feeling rejected, crying, being fearful, feeling unloved, and destructive behavior. Thus, when emotional problems of Black children were not of the acting-out variety, they tended to be overlooked. This was not true for White children and it is unlikely that this type of predisposition on the part of teachers is limited to the subjects of the Shectman study.

Although most psychiatric diagnoses of mental disorder among Blacks are made on the basis of subjective interpretations of verbal and other behavior, the assessing of Black adjustment by means of standardized personality tests does not reduce significantly the cultural bias. Smith et al. (1978); citing research with both the Rorschach and the MMPI, demonstrated that in both objective and projective testing of Blacks, interpretations of the test results by clinicians with middle-class values may lead to erroneous conclusions. In spite of this tendency towards erroneous diagnosis and interpretation of Black psychological functioning, there are a few disorders which seem clearly to be more prevalent among Blacks than among Whites. One such ailment is hypertension, which affects twice as many Blacks as Whites in the United States and is the major cause of death among Black Americans (Smith et al., 1978). This essentially physiological disorder once was thought to be of unknown origin, but recent research has shown it to have a strongly stress-related component (Meichenbaum & Jaremko, 1983). The frustrations, tensions, and conflicts involved in constantly attempting to meet one's needs and achieve one's goals in a limited opportunity structure seem to be taking its toll on Black Americans.

Another disorder with a disproportionately Black representation is that of sleep paralysis, which is an experience of being unable to move for several seconds or minutes prior or subsequent to falling asleep (Bell, 1984). Like hypertension, this disorder is thought to be caused by the tensions and stresses related to aspects of racism.

Perhaps even more fundamental than the matter of diagnosis is the probability that the cause of the disorder may not be uncovered if the mental health worker is not aware of the relevant cultural impingements. For example, Prange and Vitols (cited in Baughman, 1971), after pointing out that depression is precipitated by a sense of loss and reporting their discovery that depression is uncommon among Southern Blacks, concluded that the lack of depression was because "the Southern Negro has less to lose and is less apt to lose it" (p. 68). Such an interpretation would be unlikely from someone more than casually familiar with the Black community and its history.

Furthermore, this finding of "low depression" is in conflict with the results of other researchers who have found frequent depression among Blacks (e.g. Grier & Cobbs, cited in Baughman, 1971).

Because of this record of minsinterpreting the psychological functioning of Blacks, some researchers have pointed out the need to relate Black behavior only to Black norms (e.g. Clark, 1965; Baughman, 1971; Barnes, 1972; Baldwin, 1981; Azibo, 1984). Considering that the normal personality of Africans is allied to interpersonalism and universal interconnectionism (see chapter 6), correctly assessed Black mental illness, except for organic disorders, would seem to be related to one or more of the following: (1) failure in establishing interpersonalism, (2) failure in maintaining interpersonalism, or (3) failure in reestablishing interpersonalism once it is interrupted. Moreover, the lack of interpersonal contact as a cause of psychological distress is not a new concept. Weiss (1973) has suggested that for people in general, the inability to establish or reestablish significant relationships with other people is the basic cause of depression. This view holds that the first reaction to the absence of significant others is loneliness, and according to Weiss:

> Loneliness is a reaction to the absence of significant others based on mechanisms which once may have contributed to the survival of the species and which still are critical to the well-being of individuals. We become lonely because it is in our nature to be lonely when our lives are without certain significant relationships, just as it is in our nature to react to other deficit situations with hunger or with chill. (P. 37)

Explaining further, he tells us that in the distant past, it was essential for the survival of our primitive ancestors that they possess skills for establishing and maintaining proximity to other people. To become separated from others, especially for children, meant that the organism would have no shelter and no food. It also meant that there would be no one to care for the individual in the case of sickness or injury, and he or she would also be easy prey for the large carnivores. The presence of others promoted safety, security, and a sense of well-being. On the other hand, the intense discomfort of loneliness served as a defense against the scattering of individuals. The separated individual had to reestablish proximity, and he searched desperately to do so. When separated the individual had to communicate distress and to broadcast the necessary appeals that would result in reestablishing the proximity. When efforts at reestablishing failed, the individual developed anxiety, and if still no linkage was made after a period of time, depression set in. The relationship between depression and isolation from others is also pointed out by Freedman et al., (1972) who explain the symptoms of anaclitic depression shown by infants who are deprived of a mothering figure. These infants initially cry and struggle; then they may stop eating and waste away, eventually dying. It is possible that this explanation of loneliness, anxiety, and depression provided by Weiss and supported by Freedman et al., rather than relating only to depression and anxiety, may also explain a wide range of additional disorders and maladjustments. This is particularly true for the Black race whose African-based, strongly interpersonal predisposition has been identified. It may be, then, that many if not most of the symptoms of personal and social disorganization in the Black community (mental illness, family instability, Black-on-Black crime, substance abuse, suicide, etc.) are traceable to those Blacks who have failed either to establish, maintain, or reestablish meaningful interpersonal relationships. Obviously, much research is needed in this area before a more definitive statement can be made. However, the work of Baldwin (1981) and Baldwin & Bell (1985), discussed in chapter 6, would seem to give us a soundly-based, theoretical starting point from which empirical investigation might begin.

CHAPTER TEN

Helping Troubled Blacks

Woke up this morning feeling sad and blue
Woke up this morning feeling sad and blue
Didn't have nobody to tell my troubles to
(Blues Ballad)

Although many of the underlying causes of mental health problems among blacks may be biological, probably most are due to environmental-experiential factors. A study comparing Black and White schizophrenics found that the Black subjects improved more with a placebo, while Whites improved more with medication (Goldberg, 1966). This caused the author to conclude that psychosis in Blacks is due to psychological stress, while in Whites it is traceable to genetic factors. Ironically, psychiatric services assume that Blacks are less accessible to psychotherapy (Maas, 1967), and Black schizophrenics are "given only drugs as treatment 50% more often than whites, while receiving psychotherapy less than half as often" (Singer, cited in Bagley, 1968, p. 346). Singer also found that because the physicians were not optimistic about the responses of Blacks to treatment, the Blacks were discharged more quickly than the Whites. The racism institutionalized within the mental health profession (Thomas & Sillen, 1972) seems to suggest that psychotherapy is a treatment approach to which most Blacks are not amendable. Psychotherapy is "a form of treatment for problems of an emotional nature in which a trained person deliberately establishes a professional relationship with a patient with the object of removing, modifying, or retarding existing symptoms, of mediating disturbed patterns of behavior, and of promoting positive personality growth and development" (Wolberg, 1954, p. 3). Wolberg believes further that by calling the approach "counseling," "reeducation," or "guidance," one merely describes what happens during the course of treatment but does not dilute the therapeutic nature of the process. Most forms of psychotherapy require motivation and participation on the part of the client, as well as an elevated level of verbalization. Some practitioners also believe that superior intelligence is required. In fact, one specific approach is said to require a client I.Q. of at least 120 (Janda & Klenke-Hamel, 1982). Such a requirement would eliminate approximately 90 percent of the general population and about 98 percent of all Blacks. Signifcantly, most minority clients who seek mental health services come from the lower socioeconomic class (Smith et al., 1978). However, procedures which are less elitist are so varied and individual differences among Blacks and so vast that it is impossible to indicate the general effectiveness of psychotherapy for an entire subculture (Smith et al., 1978). However, there are strong suggestions that Blacks generally are deprived of the opportunity for maximum benefit because of the contravening attitudes, beliefs, and behavior on the part of therapists. Because, traditionally, the overwhelming majority of both clients and providers of mental health services have been White, virtually all of the theoretical formulations, research, and actual practice have been in connection with the White therapist–White client interaction. With the recent increase in Blacks who seek mental health services and the enhanced representation of Blacks as service providers, three other therapist-client diads are beginning to be recognized: (1) Black client–White therapist, (2) Black client–Black therapist, and (3) White client–Black therapist (Griffith, 1977). These "atypical" interactions are beginning to pose problems for therapists who have not been trained to deal with these types of interactions.

Racial Factors in Psychological Intervention

White Therapist–Black Client

Usually, it is expected that psychotherapists, through either rigorous self-examination or formal analysis, will have cleansed themselves of any and all attitudes and behavior that may impede the quality of the treatment process. But these therapists, overwhelmingly White, have absorbed from their culture the many prejudices, stereotypes, and other attitudes which consciously or unconsciously militate against the effective treatment of Black people (Smith et al., 1978). Effective treatment includes the presence, in the treatment relationship, of the three therapist attitudes that several studies have found to be crucial to the psychotherapeutic relationship; genuineness, accurate empathy, and non-possessive warmth (Truax & Mitchell, cited in Griffith, 1977). In a further assessment of the Black patient–White therapist diad, Smith et al. (1978) state that:

> A number of black scholars have delineated the racism found in mental-health settings and have argued that these settings are microcosms of the racism found in other spheres of American society. A number of variables that interfere with the minority client–white therapist relationship have been identified in the literature. Some of these are: (1) the inability of white psychotherapists to comprehend the social, economic, and cultural customs of blacks; (2) lack of emphasis or awareness of the therapists' own feelings regarding race and class; (3) minimal scientific research on the particulars of black and minority behaviors; (4) utilization of theoretical constructs designed by and for whites to treat black patients; and (5) clinical training that is culturally deficient in that it does not communicate a black or minority mental-health perspective. (P. 148)

One investigator sees as the primary problem in Black client–White therapist relationships the fact that "White therapists often are unable to transcend the parameters of the dominant cultural reference points" (Banks, cited in Smith et al., 1978, p. 149). The excellent review of the literature on psychotherapy with Blacks provided by Smith et al., indicates that in both inpatient and outpatient clinics, negative racial attitudes on the part of therapists "may destroy the entire therapy process from the time the client comes in the door until the client is released" (p. 150). These authors cite studies indicating that Blacks are dealt with unfairly by the mental health delivery system primarily because psychotherapists, due to their concepts of what is desirable or even acceptable in a client, tend psychologically to reject Black subjects. Additionally, because of misinformation about, lack of experience with, or complete ignorance of the Black community and its inhabitants, most psychotherapists are deficient in rapport and communication with their Black clients. Hence, there is the probability that White psychotherapists, at least unconsciously, may carry deleterious racial attitudes and practices into the treatment session, even in spite of attempts not to do so. The acutely aware American citizen now recognizes that the "melting pot" concept, though a laudable ideal is essentially a myth when applied to Black people (Baratz, 1971). One investigator, commenting on this problem, has observed that:

> Central to the problems of irreconcilable conflicts is the failure of recognition of a fundmental and obvious truth of American

> life—that the two races are residents of two separate and naturally antagonistic worlds. No manner of well-meaning rhetoric about "one country" and "one people" and even about the two race's long joint-occupancy of this troubled land can obliterate the high, thick dividing walls which hate and history have erected—and maintained—between them. The breaking down of those barriers might be a goal, worthy or unworthy (depending on viewpoint), but the reality remains. (Fuller, 1971, p. 7)

Because psychotherapy is not a culture-free activity, it is not surprising that White culture–Black culture "clashes" actually do occur in treatment, and serve to contaminate the intervention process (Griffith, 1977). Because of the pervasiveness and revocatory influences of the negative attitudes towards Blacks, some investigators (cited in Azibo, 1984) have promulgated the notion, shared by many, that White therapists are incapable of conducting effective psychotherapy with Black clients. However, the overwhelming majority of psychologists, psychiatrists, and other mental health workers are White; moreover, many of the relatively few Black providers of such services unfortunately may harbor the same harmful attitudes as do their White counterparts. Hence, the selection and referral of clients on the basis of race would seem to be a premature option. Such an eventuality would cause a crippling reduction in psychotherapeutic services for the Black community. Arguably, the complete absence of therapy may be superior to harmful therapy, but, on balance, reducing the harm seems to be more efficacious.

In reducing the harm, therapists will need to discard their theories and become more knowledgeable about the culture of their clients (Freedman, cited in Griffith, 1977). However, even this approach is fraught with hidden dangers. In viewing Black culture, the therapist may assume the culture to be the same as White culture, thereby succumbing to the "color-blindness illusion" and responding to the Black client non-differentially. This tends to deny the importance of the client's blackness and its dual impact on the psychotherapeutic process. It also may deny the therapist's whiteness and its dual impact. In addition, such denial may cause the racial barrier between client and therapist to be exacerbated and the realistic influence of racism to be overlooked. However, adopting the attitude that Black culture is contaminated by racism and oppression may cause the illusion that Black culture is permanently scarred with a "mark of oppression" (Kardiner & Oversey, 1951). From this view, all of the problems of the Black client are seen as traceable to racial discrimination. Such a view prevents the therapist from establishing a working relationship with the client, and may cause some therapists, through guilt, to offer the client special privileges and unacceptably relaxed standards of behavior (Griffith, 1977). Griffith tells us additionally that this "mark of oppression" may cause the client to believe also that all of his problems stem from racial oppression. The possible defenses of the psychotherapist could obfuscate clinical objectivity and might camouflage the client's pathological problems. Hence, therapists should neither deny the debilitating effects of racism nor be overwhelmed by the realities of this phenomenon, if clinical objectivity and maximal therapeutic effectiveness are to be held in ascendance.

These pitfalls may be avoided if the knowledge and understanding of the client and the client's community involve the normal values, standards, traditions, and customs imparted by the Black culture. The qualitative aspects of one's culture, as well as the distinctions between and among cultures, often are revealed in language and communication style (Folb, 1980). Also, language is the primary means of communication in most psychotherapeutic procedures and serves as a critical basis for the formulation, modification, and reinforcement of attitudes between therapist and client. Therefore, we should recognize that differential language usage can create an unidentified impediment to the psychotherapeutic process. Much of this negative influence may be due to the unconscious and nonverbal communication emanating from the belief that Black speech is really incorrect English and is therefore another manifestation of Black inferiority. However, as pointed out in chapter 2, there seems to be no factual basis for this point of view.

Although language and speech patterns, especially vocabulary, have been identified as major distinguishing factors in Black communication, there exist other aspects of verbal expressiveness which are uniquely characteristic of Blacks. One such trait is the call-and-response interaction. As pointed out in chapter 1, this form of communication, though most thoroughly maintained in the Black church, is found in most aspects of Black culture that require speaker-listener interrelationships (Smitherman, 1977). Hence, the term "right on" is the secular equivalent of the familiar "amen" and equally serves the communicative relationship. Other secular responses to the various "calls" in the Black community are: "dig it," "tell it," "rap on," "get down," "go 'head," "look out," "teach, teach," "hip me," and the like (Smitherman, 1977, p. 106) Furthermore, Smitherman tells us that in speaker-audience situations it is a quite acceptable means of acknowledgement for responders to make comments of approval not only to the speaker but also to each other (including whooping and ollering) while the speaker is talking. This is in marked contrast) the expectations of speaker-audience behavior in White, middle-lass culture.

In addition to the verbal responses of approval, there are nonver-al communicative reactions. Such behavior as "slapping five," rais-ig clenched fists, laughing out loud (in agreement, not in humor), tc., all serve as sanction and endorsement of the speaker's remarks Smitherman, 1977). Even in two-way communication, the partners re expected to "talk back" to each other in an active fashion, as idication of agreement and/or sympathetic understanding. As one cholar resports, "The listener acts as an echo chamber, repeating, osigning, validating and affirming the message of the speaker with mens, right-ons, yes sirs, teach-ons and you ain't never lieds. During his call-response dialogue, the speaker and listener are joined together 1 a common psycholinguistic space" (White, 1984, p. 35). Clearly, simple nod of the head can serve most deleteriously, no matter ow well-intentioned. Smitherman points out that in Black-White in-eractions, the White person fails to participate in the response process nd tends to relate passively, except for an occasional nasal utterance. 'his causes the Black person to assume that the White person is ot listening and to seek positive or negative verifications. The verbal eeking behavior annoys the White person, who because he is listen-ng, regards the "seeking" as ridiculous. On the other hand, if the Vhite person takes over the "call," the Black begins to respond so nergetically that the White person regards it as interruption and . sign that the Black person is not listening. White counselors, herapists, teachers, and others who interact with Blacks in a listening-peaking relationship discover that their cross-cultural communi-ations maybe greatly facilitated as a function of their sensitivity to his critical aspect of the Black interactional style.

3lack Client–Black Therapist

Research has shown that Black clients tend to prefer Black counselors ind psychotherapists (Banks, Berenson, & Carkhuff, 1967; Heffernon & Bruehl, 1971; GArdner, 1971; Harrison, 1977) and also tend to iave a more positive relationship (as well as outcome) when the thera-pist is Black (Philips, cited in Bryson & Bardo, 1975; Griffith, 1977). Iowever, it has been only very recently that the Black counselor–Black client relationship has been examined, and this newly-sprung issessment has not yet developed a strongly scientific foundation. Nevertheless, there seem to be both positive and negative aspects of Black client–Black therapist interaction, as pointed out by Griffith

(1977). The similarity in racial background should, and often does facilitate the relationship. Yet, this very similarity may be the caus of many adverse effects. For example, as a function of contagiou bias, the client may equate blackness with inferiority and thereb reject the therapist as one who is less capable than a White therapis On the other hand, the client may perceive the therapist as one wh has overcome great odds to reach an elevated professional status thereby demonstrating the therapist's superiority. By contrast, th client may view herself as inadequate and inferior.

Because feeling about blackness are critical to the therapist as we as to the client, any denial of blackness on the part of the therapis may cause him or her to reject the client, whose presence and behavic may prove to be an unbearable threat. In contrast with this probler of rejection is the matter of over-identification, where the therapis strongly accepts his own blackness and "over-involves himself in th socio-economic aspects of the client's problems" (Griffith, 1977, p 34). As a consequence, the therapist may over-participate in the cl ent's etiological view of his or her conflicts and stresses, causin basic issues to be obscured. Hence, the therapist must deal wit aspects of Black identity within himself as well as within his client This difficulty has caused Seward and Von Tress (cited in Griffith 1977) to claim that the Black client may encounter *more* problem when the therapist is Black than when he or she is White. Howeve as Griffith points out, there is no evidence to support this assertior

Black Therapist–White Client

There are very few scientific investigations of the relationship betwee Black therapists and White clients, probably because of the relativ scarcity of Black mental health professionals. However, the existin studies reveal that the race of the therapist does indeed affect th intervention relationship (Griffith, 1977). Citing the works of suc investigators as Curry, Banks, Carkhuff and Pierce, Gardner and Jack son; and also drawing upon the theory of cognitive dissonance, Griffit shows that "engrained societal attitudes of black inferiority are no checked in the waiting room when the white client enters treatmen with a black therapist" (p. 36). Some White clients may refuse t enter treatment with a Black therapist, or may terminate treatmen prematurely, once entered. Those who do engage a Black therapis may manifest an attitude of superiority and demonstrate a postur of patronization. Other White clients unrealistically may deny th color difference, while still others may assume the Black therapist' "blackness" to have been obliterated by the process of his professiona lization. An additional response is for the White client to be oversolicitous toward the Black therapist, who the client views as being gravely burdened with problems much greater than those of the client. According to Curry (cited in Griffith, 1977), this situation can create insurmountable obstacles in treatment. On the other hand, the Black therapist–White client interaction may have beneficial effects on the therapeutic process, since there may be an accelerted uncovering of essential problems as a consequence of exposed racial feelings (Schacter & Butts, cited in Griffith, 1977).

A few investigators have argued that the limitations occasioned by these various interracial diads can be overcome by adopting a culture-fair model of dynamic psychotherapy (Tyler et al., 1985). Such a model would evolve out of the therapist's recognition of the multiethnic reality of the world, the wide variations in ways of "being human," and the relative validity of each ethnic group's values and world-views. The debate on this matter has just begun, but thus far the consensus seems to be that the psychodynamic tradition holds little promise of becoming culture-fair.

Non-racial Variables in the Pyschotherapeutic Relationship

In addition to the influence on the psychotherapeutic relationship of such factors as client and therapist attitudes, beliefs, and values, as occasioned by race, are the effects of the theoretical orientation of the therapist, the interaction model employed, and the overall structure and process of the therapy session. Although most of these factors have received little attention in the professional literature, and virtually none have been the subject of rigid experimental treatment, attention should be called to what has been formulated thus far.

The therapist's theoretical orientation is critical, since it influences the type of model used and determines the structure and process of the sessions. Because nearly all psychotherapists, including those of African heritage, have been indoctrinated in Eurocentric theories, Africentric theories of personality development and maladjustment only recently have begun to emerge. The observations of Nobles (1980), Baldwin (1981), and Williams (1981), as well as the formulation presented by the present author in chapters 6 and 8 of this volume, all indicate that an understanding of the Black personality requires a thorough grasp of basic African antecedents.

Because of the preponderance of Eurocentric theories of mental illness, most psychological intervention models are also Eurocentric. Hence, the Rational-Emotive Therapy of Albert Ellis, the Client-

Centered or Nondirective Therapy of Carl Rogers, the Cognitive Therapy of Aaron Beck, and especially the psychoanalysis of Sigmund Freud, are of questionable value in providing maximal treatment benefits to Black clients. Commenting on this matter, Jackson (1976) responds that the "do-it-yourself aspect of the nondirective approach is seen as threatening to the client and may result in the client's withdrawal" (p. 297). He also views psychoanalysis to be unsuitable in an African setting and regards even the behavior therapy approach, though having many advantages, to be in need of widespread overhaul before being applied to an African setting. A much more promising outlook for behavior therapy is seen by Maultsby (1982), who considers this approach to be culture-free and thus minimally biased against Blacks. By "culture-free" Maultsby means that the approach is equally effective for Blacks, Whites, and others, regardless of age, sex, or socioeconomic status. He further concludes that in the United States the specifically most effective techniques for Blacks are those of classical behavior therapy, cognitive behavior therapy, and rational behavior therapy.

African Personality as a Factor in the Helping Process

In view of the uniqueness of the Black personality, discussed in chapter 6, it is likely that treatment approaches based on African interpersonalism and/or African self-extension orientation might be more effective than any other theoretical application in dealing with Black patients and clients. African interpersonalism suggests that the need for meaningful contact with others is present in all Blacks and that its gratification is positively correlated with psychological adjustment. Thus, a "disturbed," "abnormal," or "maladjusted" Black individual would be one who, due to environmental impediments, has experienced either a curtailment or a thwarting of the normal drive towards interpersonalism. Because such interpersonalism involves not only affiliation with but also concern for and subordination to other people, it is closely allied to the African self-extension orientation. Validly operative psychotherapy, then, should be directed towards reestablishing the strength and facilitating the realization of this basic urge. There is even some recent suggestion that moving in the direction of interpersonalism might have positive results for *all* people, not merely those of African descent. For example, Ornstein and Sobel (1987) have discovered that the immune system appears to be strengthened when an individual is thinking about someone or something other than himself or herself. Additionally, Seligman (cited in Buie,

1988) reports that since World War II, more people have suffered depression as a result of an enhanced commitment to the self and a reduced commitment to family, community, nation, and religion. "Traditional institutions, Seligman said, despite their demands for conformity, buffered people when they failed and kept them from sinking into despair" (Buie, 1988, p. 18). Buie also quotes Seligman as saying that hopelessness, low self-esteem, etc., were not found in non-Western cultures before they were modernized and that in less Westernized cultures, depression may be completely absent. Because of the Africans' intense focus on interpersonalism, it would seem that they and their descendants would be most affected by individualistic focalizations and that effective psychotherapy should be directed towards restoring the social bonding. The question of whether current psychotherapeutic techniques, with modification, are suitable for this task must be left to future research for a meaningful answer.

However, several theorists have suggested that regardless of the therapist's theoretical model or treatment orientation, the structure and process of the therapy sessions may be the primary cause of ineffective treatment with Blacks (Bryson & Bardo, 1975). For example, Calia (cited in Bryson & Bardo, 1975) has raised questions about sedentary talk as a medium for client-counselor interaction, unconditional positive regard as an essential therapeutic element, and facilitation of self-exploration as a goal of counseling. Other authors, along with Calia, have called for action-oriented treatment approaches, which focus on external factors and emphasize assisting the client with the environmental manipulation. This new thrust is in response to the recognition that many of the Black client's problems are caused by his failed attempts in dealing with unjust environmental restrictions. In this regard, the traditionally intrapsychic model is viewed as being invalid as an interaction technique for Black people. In fact, many Blacks may feel that they are being discriminated against if talk is substituted for more tangible evidence of treatment (Baughman, 1971; Gardner, 1971). In Africa, the medicine man, witch doctor, and priest all have overlapping functions (Mbiti, 1969), most of which involved ministering to people's physical and emotional ills in a direct, active, and overt fashion. Hence, the expectation is that the "doctor" will do something specific and observable in treating the patient's problems. One possible solution is to focus on group therapy, which facilitates the interpersonalism and the "extended family" orientation of African culture. The security, support, and suggestions offered by the therapy group may serve most beneficially in helping the client learn how to deal more effectively with environmental impingements.

Rigidly structured appointment schedules may serve as an additional barrier to a good therapeutic relationship, because they are antithetical to the events-based concept of time which is characteristic of Black culture. Such inflexibility may be perceived as rejection, lack of genuine caring, or a symptom of insensitivity to cultural differences.

One must also recognize that because of psychiatry's and psychology's negative view and treatment of Blacks in the past, present-day Blacks have an understandable distrust of mental health professionals (Maultsby, 1982). In addition, Maultsby reminds us that Blacks tend to hold a bipolar view of mental health. At one extreme are emotionally normal people who solve their own problems, and at the other end are "crazy" people who must have the assistance of psychiatrists and other mental health workers. The basic distrust coupled with the aversion to being labeled "crazy" seems to reduce the probability that many Black clients will be "self-referrals." As Jackson (1976) explains, "A professional will need to go out and bring in for therapy those who may have problems but are either unaware that they do or are for some reason unwilling to refer themselves" (p. 6). Africans, when contacted in this manner, are far less likely to regard it as an interference in their private affairs, because similar situations are an everyday occurence in African life. The same seems to be true of Black Americans.

Once the racial, theoretical, structural, and procedural problems are solved, one should expect the beginning stages of therapy with Blacks to be relatively easy, because of the client's desire to help others and the expectation that others will want to help the client (care syndrome). During this initial phase, the effects of discrimination should be considered and the client should be helped in learning how to deal with these consequences. Often a good prognosis for a Black client means the ability to bring about change in the American system. Thus, self-realization for Black clients may demand that the therapist help them to become effective agents of social change. As a function of the care syndrome, peers and significant others should be involved in the overall process as much as possible.

But most basic for effective psychological intervention with Blacks is a thorough understanding of African personality development, something that is lacking on the part of most mental health workers. Africentric interpersonalism or the more global African self-extension orientation, discussed in chapter 6, are seldom (if ever) considered in the diagnoses, prognoses, treatment goals, and intervention strategies regarding Black patients and clients. A major reason for this predicament is that most training programs for mental health workers, in spite of many recently developed good faith efforts, are woefully lacking in the relevant information and therefore have no basis for the much-needed dissemination. The sensitive therapist, however, should recognize that the two cultures, Black and White, had existed separately and apart in geographically isolated environments for centuries before the first intercultural and interracial contacts were made. It is thus understandable that there exist many cognitive, affective, behavioral, and overall cosmological characteristics that are peculiar to each group. Effective psychotherapy would seem to involve accepting and relating to these differences in such a way as to enhance the intervention process without being either haunted by the inferiority-superiority specter or restricted by a lack of understanding regarding the Africentric focus. One means of addressing the problem might be to enlist the assistance of knowledgeable persons in the integration of relevant material on minorities into the professional training curricula. In addition, practica, internships, externships, and programs for continuing education should be planned so as to include significant training in effective intervention with Black and other minority clients and patients.

More than focusing on the Black client, training programs, in order to be maximally effective and sensitive, should be designed to consider the needs, values, and perceptions of Black and other minority trainees. In this connection, Thomas (cited in Smith et al.) indicates four problems encountered by Blacks who enter training programs in psychology: (1) irrelevance of content; (2) obsolescence of methods; (3) failure to build in present assumptions about the nature of humanity; and (4) reluctance to bring action to bear on social issues that confront the larger society (Smith et al., 1978, p. 133). Many of these problems, according to Leggett (cited in Smith et al., 1978) are occasioned by the fact that minority students have a greater desire to use psychological training as a means of effective change in the conditions that produce oppression. Underscoring this point, Smith et al. tell us that minority students desire to focus on procedures that are functionally relevant to problems that are faced by minority groups. These students, therefore, seek professional training and education that are not only action-oriented but also are directed towards the explication of minority subjugation. The authors further state that:

> When the Black student is in a graduate program that is not action-oriented and does not include minority contributions in theory and research as part of the curriculum, then the program may be viewed as irrelevant and obsolete. In order

> to circumvent these and other criticisms of training minorities in psychology, it will be necessary to plan and implement new types of training programs, as well as to revise existing training programs to answer the mental health needs of minority communities. (1978, p. 133)

The observation by Green (cited in Smith et al.) that minority students should learn how to diagnose and correct the social and institutional causes of human suffering, rather than being limited to minority students, would seem to apply to all mental health workers in the Black community, regardless of race or professional level. Two programs that seem to have this social focus are the Urban Counseling Mental Health Program at Michigan State University and the Minority Mental Health Program in Psychology at Washington University in St. Louis, Missouri. Both of these programs, through research theory and practice, expose the students to minority mental health issues, with the expectation that their academic training will be applied to real-life minority concerns, the effectiveness of these programs should encourage other colleges and universities to move in a similar direction.

References

Anastasi, A. (1968). *Psychological testing.* New York: MacMillan.

Anastasi, A. (1981). *Psychological testing.* New York: MacMillan.

Andrews, M. & Owens, P. T. (1973). *Black language.* Los Angeles: Seymour-Smith.

Asinof, E. (1970). *People vs. Blutcher.* New York: Viking.

Association of Black Psychologists. (1984). *Information brochure.* Washington, DC: Author.

Azibo, D.A.Y. (1984). *Advances in Black personality theory.* Paper presented at the 17th Annual Convention of the Association of Black Psychologists, New York, August 10, 1984.

Bagley, C. (1968). Migration race and mental health: A review of some recent research. *Race IX*(3), 343-356.

Baldwin, J. (1976). Black psychology and Black personality. *Black Books Bulletin, 4*(3), 6–11.

Baldwin, J. A. (1981). Notes on an Africentric theory of Black personality. *Western Journal of Black Studies, 5,* 172–179.

Baldwin, J. A. & Bell, Y. R. (1985). The African self-consciousness scale: An African personality questionnaire. *Western Journal of Black Studies,* 9(2), 61–68.

Bandura, A., & Walters, A. (1963). *Social learning and personality development.* New York: Holt, Reinhart & Winston.

Banks, G. P., Berenson, B. G., & Carkhoff, R. R. (1967). The effects of counselor race and training upon counseling process with Negro clients in initial interviews. *Journal of Clinical Psychology, 23,* 70–72.

Banks, H. A. (1970). Black consciousness: A student survey. *Black Scholar, 2* (1), 44–51.

Baratz, J. C. (1971, Spring/Fall). "Ain't" ain't no error. *Florida FL Reporter,* pp. 39–41.

Barnes, E. J. (1972). Cultural retardation or shortcomings of assessment techniques? In R. Jones (Ed.), *Black psychology.* New York: Harper & Row.

Baskin, D., Bluestone, H., & Nelson, M. (1981). Ethnicity and psychiatric diagnosis. *Journal of Clinical Psychology, 39,* 529–537.

Baughman, E. E. (1971). *Black Americans.* New York: Academic Press.

Beck, A. T. (1974). Depressive neurosis. In S. Arieti (Ed.), *American Handbook of Psychiatry.* New York: Basic Books.

Bell, C. C. (1984). Prevalence of isolated sleep paralysis in Black subjects. *Journal of the National Medical Association, 76*(5), 501–508.

Biesheuvel, S. (1943). *African intelligence.* Johannesburg: South African Institute of Race Relations.

Black Psychologists Today. (1978). Washington, DC: Association of Black Psychologists.

Blackwell, J. E. (1985). *The Black community.* New York: Harper & Row.

Blauner, R. (1972). *Racial oppression in America.* New York: Harper & Row.

Boring, E. G. (1929). *A history of experimental psychology.* New York: D. Appleton-Century.

Boyd, W. M. (1977, November). SATs and minorities: The dangers of underprediction. *Change,* pp. 48–49; 64.

Boykin, A. W., Franklin, A. J., & Yates, J. F. (1979). Work notes on empirical research in Black psychology. In A. W. Boykin, A. J. Franklin and J. F. Yates (Eds.), *Research directions of Black psychologists.* New York: Russell Sage Foundation.

Brandt, R. B. (1954). *Hopi ethics.* Chicago: University of Chicago Press.

Breed, W. (1967). Suicide and loss in social interaction. In E. S. Schneidman (Ed.), *Essays in self-destruction.* New York: Science House.

Breed, W. (1970). The Negro and fatalistic suicide. *Pacific Sociological Review, 13,* 156–162.

Brodie, H.K.H. (1973). The effects of ethyl alcohol in man. In National Commission on Marijuana and Drug Abuse, *Drug use in America: Problems in perspective* (pp. 6–59).

Bryson, S., & Bardo, H. (1975). Race and the counseling process: an overview. *Journal of Non-White Concerns in Personnel and Guidance, 4*(1), 5–15.

Buie, J. (1988, October). "Me" decades generate depression. *APA Monitor,* p. 18.

Burke, A. W. (1974). Socio-cultural aspects of attempted suicide among women in Trinidad and Tobago. *Brit. J. of Psychiatry, 125,* 374–377.

Burkey, R. M. (1978). *Ethnic and racial groups.* Menlo Park, Ca. Cumming.

Caetano, R. (1984). Ethnicity and drinking in northern California. A comparison among Whites, Blacks and Hispanics. *Alcohol and Alcoholism, 19*(1), 31–34.

Chamberlain, B. H.(1927). *Things Japanese.* London: Paul, Trench, Trubner.

Chance, P. (1975). Race and IQ: A family affair? *Psychology Today, 8* (8), 40.

Chance, P. (1981). The remedial thinker. *Psychology Today, 15*(10), 63–73.

Chaplin, J. P. (1975). *Dictionary of psychology.* New York: Dell.

Clark, K. B. & Clark, M. P. (1950). Emotional factors in racial identification and preference in Negro children. *Journal of Negro Education, 19,* 341–350.

Clark, K. (1965). *Dark ghetto.* New York: Harper & Row.

Cleaver, E. (1968). *Soul on ice.* New York: McGraw-Hill.

Coleman, J. C. (1964). *Abnormal psychology and modern life.* Glenview, Illinois: Scott, Foresman.

Comer, J. P. (1972). *Beyond Black and White.* New York: Quadrangle Books.

Crain, R. L., & Weisman, C. S. (1972). *Discrimination, personality and achievement.* New York: Seminar Press.

Crawford, G. A., Washington, M. C. & Senay, E. C. (1983). Careers with heroin. *International Journal of the Addictions, 18*(5), 701–715.

Crime: The deadliest city. (1973, January 1). *Newsweek,* pp. 20–21.

Darley, J. M., Glucksberg, S., Kamin, L. J., & Kinchla, R. A. (1984). *Psychology.* Englewood Cliffs, NJ.

DaSilva, B. (1969). *The Afro-American in United States history.* New York: Globe Book Company.

Davidson, B. (1961). *Black mother: The years of the African slave trade.* Boston: Little, Brown.

Davis, K. (1947). Final note on a case of extreme isolation. *American Journal of Sociology, 45,* 554-565.

Dawkins, R. L., & Dawkins, M. P. (1983). Alcohol use and delinquency among Black, White and Hispanic adolescent offenders. *Adolescence, 18*(72), 799-809.

Dent, H. E. (1980, Spring). Facts on Larry P. *Association of Black Psychologists Newsletter,* pp. 14–16.

Dialect of the Black American. (1970). New York: Western Electric.

Dillard, J. D. (1972). *Black English.* New York: Random House.

Dobzhansky, T. (1973). Differences are not deficits. *Psychology Today,* December, 96–106.

Does race really make a difference in intelligence? (1956, October 26). *U.S. News and World Report,* pp. 74, 76.

Dollard, J. (1937). *Caste and class in a southern town.* New Haven: Yale University Press.

Dollard, J., Doob, L. W., Miller, N. E., Mowrer, O. H., & Sears, R. R. (1939). *Frustration and aggression.* New Haven: Yale University Press.

Durham, P., & Jones, E. (1965). *The Negro cowboys.* New York: Dodd Mead.

Durkheim, E. (1951). *Suicide: A study in sociology.* Glencoe: Free Press.

Edwards, A. L. (1974). *Statistical analysis.* New York: Holt, Rinehart & Winston.

Edwards, T. G. (1972). Looking back on growing up Black. In R. W. Pugh (Ed.), *Psychology and the Black experience.* Monterey, Ca.: Brooks/Cole.

Encyclopaedia Britannica. (1972a). Volume 14, p. 191. Chicago: William Benton.

Encyclopaedia Britannica. (1972b). Volume 21, pp. 1155–159. Chicago: William Benton.

English H. B., & English, A. C. (1958). *A comprehensive dictionary of psycho-analytical terms.* New York: Longmans, Dean.

Evans, B. & Waites, B. (1981): *I.Q. and mental testing.* Atlantic Highlands, N. J.: Humanities Press.

Evans, L. (1984). Self-reported psychiatric symptoms among Black, Hispanic and white outpatients. *Journal of Clinical Psychology, 40*(5), 1184–1189.

Ferguson, G. A. (1976). *Statistical analysis of psychology and education.* New York: McGraw-Hill.

Feuerstein, R. (1979). *The dynamic assessment of retarded performers: the learning potential assessment device, theory instruments and techniques.* Baltimore: University Park Press.

Folb, E. A. (1980). *Runnin' down some lines.* Cambridge, MA: Harvard University Press.

Foner, P. S. (1975). *History of Black Americans.* Westport, CT: Greenwood Press.

Frazier, E. F. (1964). *The Negro church in America.* New York: Schocken.

Freedman, A. M., Kaplan, H. I., & Saddock, B. J. (1972). *Modern synopsis of psychiatry.* Baltimore: Williams & Wilkins.

Fulks. B. (1969). *Black struggles; a history of the Negro in America.* New York: Dell.

Fuller, H. (1971). Towards a Black aesthetic. In A. Gayle (Ed.), *The Black aesthetic.* New York: Doubleday.

Garber, H., and Heber, F. R. (1977). The Milwaukee project—indications of the effectiveness of early intervention in preventing mental retardation. In P. Mittler, (Ed.), *Research in practice in mental retardation, Vol. I: care and intervention.* Baltimore: University Park Press.

Gardner, L. H. (1971). The therapeutic relationship under varying conditions of race. *Psychotherapy: Theory, Research and Practice, 8*(1), 78–87.

Garrett, H. E. (1941). *Great experiments in psychology.* New York: Appleton-Century-Crofts.

Gary, L. E., & Berry, G. L. (1984). Some determinants of attitudes toward substance use in an urban ethnic community. *Psychological Reports, 54*(2), 539–545.

Goldberg, E. (1966). Sex and race differences in response to drug treatment among schizophrenics. *Psychopharmacologia, 9*, 31–47.

Goldschmid, M. L. (1970). *Black Americans and white racism.* New York: Holt, Rinehart and Winston.

Goleman, D., Egen, T., & Davids, A. (1982). *Introductory psychology.* New York: Random House.

Gordon, M. (1964). *Assimilation in American life.* New York: Basic Books.

Gould, S. J. (1981). *The mismeasure of man.* New York: W.W. Norton.

Grayzel, S. (1947). *A history of the Jews.* Philadelphia: The Jewish Publication Society of America.

Greenfield, P. M., & Bruner, J. S. (1971). Learning and language: Work with the Wolof. *Psychology Today, 5*(2) 40–43; 74; 76; 78–79.

Grier, W. H. & Cobbs, P. M. (1968). *Black Rage*. New York: Basic Books.

Grier, W. H. & Cobbs, P. M. (1970). If the black man comes unglued. In R. V. Guthrie (Ed.). *Being Black*. San Francisco: Canfield Press.

Griffith, M. S. (1977). The influence of race on the psychotherapeutic relationship. *Psychiatry, 40*(1), 27–40.

Grossack, M. M. (1957). Some personality characteristics of Southern Negro students. *Journal of Social Psychology, 46*, 125–131.

Grossack, M. M. (1963). *Mental health and segregation*. New York: Springer.

Guthrie, R. V. (1970). *Being Black: Psychological-sociological dilemmas*. San Francisco: Canfield Press.

Guthrie, R. V. (1976). *Even the rat was white*. New York: Harper & Row.

Hall, C. S. & Lindzey, G. (1978). *Theories of personality*. New York: John Wiley.

Hankoff, L. D., & Einsidler, B. (1979). *Suicide theory and clinical aspects*. Littleton, MA: PSG Publishing Company.

Harper, R. S. (1949). Tables of American doctorates in psychology. *American Journal of Psychology, 62*, 579–587.

Harrison, D. K. (1977). The attitudes of Black counselees toward White counselors. *Journal of Non-White Concerns in Personnel and Guidance, 5*(2), 52–59.

Hastorf, A. H., & Cantril, H. (1954). They saw a game: A case study. *Journal of Abnormal and Social Psychology, 49*, 129–134.

Hatton, C. L., Valente, S. M., & Rink, A. (1977). *Suicide assessment and intervention*. New York: Appleton-Century-Crofts.

Hauze, B. (1977). Suicide: Special references to Black women. *Journal of Non-White Concerns in Personnel and Guidance, 5*(2), 65–72.

Hendin, H. (1969). *Black Suicide*. New York: Basic Books.

Heffernon, A., Bruehl, D. (1971). Some effects of race of inexperienced lay counselors on Black junior high school students. *Journal of School Psychology, 9*(1), 35–37.

Herskovits, M. J. (1935). Social history of the Negro. in C. Murchison (Ed.), *A handbook of social psychology*. (pp. 207–267). Worchester, MA: Clark University Press.

Hinsie, L. E., & Campbell, R. J. (1970). *Psychiatric dictionary*. New York: Oxford University Press.

Houston, L. N. (1980). Predicting academic achievement among specially admitted Black female undergraduates. *Eductional and Psychological Measurement, 40*(4), 1189–1195.

Houston, L. N. (1982). Black consciousness among female undergraduates at a predominantly White college: 1973 and 1979. *Journal of Social Psychology*, 118, 289-290.

Houston, L. N. (1983). The comparative predictive validities of high school rank, the Ammons Quick Test and two scholastic aptitude measures for a sample of Black female college students. *Educational and Psychological Measurement, 43*(4), 1123–1126.

Houston, L. N. (1987). The preductive validity of a study habits inventory for first semester undergraduates. *Eductional and Psychological Measurement, 47,* 1025–1030.

Humphrey, J. A., Stephens, V., & Allen, D. F. (1983). Race, sex, marijuana use and alcohol intoxication in college students. *Journal of Studies on Alcohol, 44*(4), 733-738.

Hunt, W. A. (1947). The relative incidence of psychoneurosis among Negroes. *Journal of Consulting Psychology, 11,* 133–136.

Jackson, G. (1976). The African genesis of the Black perspective in helping. *Professional Psychology, 7*(3), 292–308.

Janda, L. H., & Klenke-Hamel, K. E. (1982). *Psychology.* New York: St Martin's.

Jan-Tausch, J. (1963). *Suicide of children 1960–63. New Jersey public school students.* Trenton, N. J.: Department of Education, Office of Special Education Services.

Jenkins. A. (1982). *The psychology of the Afro-American.* New York: Pergamon.

Jensen, A. R. (1969a). How much can we boost I.Q. and scholastic achievement? *Harvard Educational Review, 39*(1), 1–123.

Jensen, A. R. (1969b). Reducing the heredity-environment uncertainty. *Harvard Educational Review, 39*(1), 209–243.

Jensen, A. R. (1980). *Bias in mental testing.* New York: Free Press.

Johnson, J. R., & Johnson, J. W. (1925). *The book of American Negro spirituals.* New York: Viking.

Jones, R. L. (Ed.) (1978). *Black psychology.* New York: Harper & Row.

Jordan, W. (1975). Voodoo medicine. In R. A. Williams (Ed.), *A textbook of Black related diseases.* New York: McGraw-Hill.

Joseph, A. (1977). *Intelligence, I.Q. and race—when, how and why they became associated.* San Francisco: R & E Research.

Kamin, L. (1974). *The science and politics of I.Q.* Potomac, MD: Lawrence Erlbaum.

Kardiner, A., & Oversey, L. (1951). *The mark of oppression.* New York: World Publishing.

Katz, W. L. (1973). *The Black West.* New York: Anchor.

Kennedy, W. A. (1971). *Child psychology.* Englewood Cliffs, NJ: Prentice-Hall.

Khoapa, B. A. (1980). *The African personality.* Japan: The United Nations University.

Kiev, A. (1979). Transcultural perspectives. In L. D. Hankoff and B. Einsidler (Eds.) *Suicide theory and clinical aspects.* Littleton, MA: PSG Publishing Company.

Kimble, G., & Garmezy, N. (1968). *Principles of general psychology.* New York: Ronald Press.

King, B. B., Why I sing the blues. In *B. B. King live & well.* Elk Grove Village, IL: Bluesway Records.

King, E. (1975). *Negro songs and singers.* Hartford, CT: American Publishing Company.

Klatsky, A. L., Siegelaub, A. B., Landry, C., & Friedman, G. D. (1983). Racial patterns of alcoholic beverage use. *Alcoholism: Clinical and Experimental Research, 7*(4), 372–377.

Layzer, D. (1976). Science or superstition? In Block, N. J. and G. Dworkin (Eds.) *The I.Q. controversy.* New York: Pantheon.

Lerner, G. (1972). *Black women in White America; a documentary history.* New York: Pantheon.

Lewin, R. (1977). Head Start pays off. *New Scientist, 73*(1041), 508–509.

Lewis, C. E., Cloniger, C. R., & Pais, J. (1983). Alcoholism, antisocial personality and drug use in a criminal population. *Alcohol and Alcoholism, 18*(1), 53–60.

Lewis, H. (1955). *Blackways of Kent.* Chapel Hill: University of North Carolina Press.

Linton, M., & Gallo, P. S. (1975). *The practical statistician: Simplified handbook of statistics.* Monterey, CA: Brooks/Cole.

Lomax, J. A., & Lomax, A. (1947). *Folk song U.S.A.* New York: Duell, Sloan & Pearce.

Lynn, R. (1982). I.Q. in Japan and the United States shows a growing disparity. *Nature, 297,* 222–223.

Malcolm X. (1965). *The last message.* Englewood, New Jersey: All Platinum Records.

Mannix, D., & Cowley, M. (1972). *Black cargoes; a history of the Atlantic slave trade, 1518–1865.* New York: Penguin Books.

Maultsby, M. C. (1982). A historical view of Blacks' distrust of psychiatry. In S. M. Turner and R. T. Jones (Eds.), *Behavior modification in Black populations.* New York: Plenum.

Mbiti, J. S. (1969). *African religions and philosophy.* New York: Praeger.

McClelland, D. (1973). Testing for competence rather than for intelligence. *American Psychologist,* 1973, 28(1), 1–14.

McGurk, F.C.J. (1956, September 21). A scientist's report on race differences. *U.S. News and World Report,* pp. 92–96.

Meeker, M. (1963). *The structure of intellect; its use and interpretation.* Columbus, OH: Charles E. Merrill.

Meichenbaum, D., & Jaremko, M. (1983). *Stress reduction and prevention.* New York: Plenum.

Mercer, J. R. (1973). *Labeling the mentally retarded.* Berkeley: University of California Press.

Mercer, J. R. (1979), *SOMPA: system of multicultural pluralistic assessment technical manual.* New York: Psychological Corporation.

Mindel, C. H., & Haberstein, R. W. (Eds.) (1976). *Ethnic Families in America.* New York: Elsevier.

Mohs, M. (1982, September). New research shows that the Japanese outperform all others in intelligence tests. Are they really smarter? *Discover,* pp. 19–24.

Montagu, A. (1963). *Race, science and humanity.* Princeton, NJ: Van Nostrand.

Morgan, M. C., Wingard, D. L., & Felice, M. E. (1984). Subcultural differences in alcohol use among youth. *Journal of Adolescent Health Care, 5*(3), 191–195.

Mullan, E. H. (1970). *Mentality of the arriving immigrant.* New York: Arno.

Myrdal, G. (1944). *An American dilemma; the Negro problem and modern democracy.* New York: Harper.

National Commission on Marijuana and Drug Abuse. (1973). *Drug use in America: Problems in perspective.* Washington, DC: U.S. Government Printing Office.

Neisser, U. (1976). *Cognition and reality: Principles and implications of cognitive psychology.* San Francisco: Freeman, Cooper.

Nobles, W. W. (1972). African philosophy: foundations for Black psychology. In R. L. Jones (Ed.), *Black psychology.* New York: Harper & Row.

Nobles, W. W. (1980). Extended self: Rethinking the so-called Negro self-concept. In R. L. Jones (Ed.), *Black psychology,* (pp. 99–105). New York: Harper & Row.

Ornstein, R. E. (1977). *The psychology of consciousness.* New York: Harcourt, Brace, Jovanovich.

Ornstein, R. E. & Sobel, D. (1987). *The healing brain.* New York: Simon & Schuster.

O'Toole, T. (1976, February 22). Panel sees no link in race, intelligence. *Sunday Times Advertiser,* p. B-11.

Parrinder, G. (1969). *Religions in Africa.* New York: Praeger.

Pasamanick, B. (1963). A survey of mental disease in an urban population. In M. M. Grossack (Ed.), *Mental health and segregation.* New York: Springer.

Peck, D. L. (1983). "Official documentation" of the Black suicide experience. *Omega: Journal of Death and Dying, 14,*(1), 21–31.

Plutchik, R., Kellerman, H., & Conte, H. R. (1979). A structural theory of ego defenses and emotions. In C. E. Izard (Ed.), *Emotions in personality and psychopathology.* New York: Plenum.

Pokorny, A. D. (1964). Suicide rates in various psychiatric disorders. *Journal of Nervous and Mental Disease, 139,* 499–506.

Porterfield, E. (1973). Mixed marriage. *Psychology Today, 6*(8), 71–72; 74–78.

Poussaint, A. (1970). A Negro psychiatrist explains the Negro psyche. In R. V. Guthrie (Ed.), *Being Black.* San Francisco: Canfield Press.

Poussaint, A. (1972). *Why Blacks kill Blacks.* New York: Emerson Hall.

Pyle, D. W. (1979). *Intelligence, an introduction.* Boston: Routledge & Kegan Paul.

Report of the national advisory commission on civil disorders. (1968). New York: Bantam.

Reynolds, D. K., Kalish, R. A., & Farbero, H. L. (1975). A cross-ethnic study of suicide attitudes and expectations in the United States. In H. L. Farberow (Ed.), *Suicide in different cultures.* Baltimore: University Park Press.

Rose, P. I. (1964). *They and we: Racial and ethnic relations in the United States.* New York: Random House.

Ruch, F. L. (1963). *Psychology and life.* Chicago: Scott.

Samuda, R. J. (1975). *Psychological testing of American minorities.* New York: Harper & Row.

Scott-Heron, G. (1974). *The revolution will not be televised.* New York: Flying Dutchman Productions.

Seiden, R. H. (1966). Campus tragedy: A study of student suicide. *Journal of Abnormal Psychology, 71*(6), 389–399.

Seiden, R. H. (1970). We are driving young Blacks to suicide. *Psychology Today, 4*(3), 24–28.

Seligman, M.E.P. (1975). *Helplessness.* San Francisco: Freeman.

Shavelsen, R. J. (1981). *Statistical reasoning for the behavioral sciences.* Boston: Allyn and Bacon.

Shechtman, A. (1971). Psychiatric symptoms observed in normal and disturbed Black children. *Journal of Clinical Psychology, 27*(4), 445–447.

Shuey, A. M. (1966). *The testing of Negro intelligence.* New York: Social Science Press.

Silberman, C. E. (1985). *A certain people.* New York: Summit.

Skinner, B. F. (1957). The experimental analysis of behavior. *American Scientist, 45,* 343–371.

Skodak, M., & Skeels, H. M. (1949). A final follow-up study of one hundred adopted children. *Journal of Genetic Psychology, 75,* 85–125.

Slack, W. V., & Porter, D. (1980). The Scholastic Aptitude Test: A critical appraisal. *Harvard Educational Review, 50*(2), 154–175.

Smith, D. H., & Hackathorn, L. (1982). Some social and psychological factors related to suicide in primitive societies: A cross-cultural comparative study. *Suicide and Life-threatening Behavior, 12*(4), 195–211.

Smith, W. D., Burlew, A. K., Mosley, M. H., & Whitney, W. M. (1978). *Minority issues in mental health.* Reading, MA.: Addison-Wesley.

Smitherman, G. (1977). *Talkin' and testifyin'.* Boston: Houghton Mifflin.

Solomon, J., and Arnon D. (1979). Alcohol and other substance abusers. In L. D. Hankoff and B. Einsidler (Eds.), *Suicide theory and clinical aspects.* (pp. 263–278). Littleton, MA: PSG Publishing Company.

Spearman, C. (1927). *The abilities of man.* London: MacMillan.

Spearman, C. (1904). General intelligence, objectively determined and measured. *American Journal of Psychology, 15,* 201–293.

Staples, R. (1976). *Introduction of Black sociology.* New York: McGraw Hill.

Stipp, D. (1985). College SATs grow in importance despite long history of criticism. *The Wall Street Journal,* February 5, p. 33.

Sullivan, H. S. (1963). Memorandum on a psychiatric reconnaissance. In M. M. Grossack (Ed.), *Mental health and segregation.* New York: Springer.

Sweetland, R. C. & Keyser, D. J. (1983). *Tests: A comprehensive reference for assessments in psychology, education, and business.* Kansas City: Test Corp. of America.

Symonds, P. M. (1949). *Dynamic Psychology.* New York: Appleton-Century-Crofts, 1949.

Taft, D. R. (1950). *Criminology: A cultural interpretation.* New York: MacMillan.

Temples, P. (1952). *Bantu philosophy.* Paris: Présence Africaine.

Thomas, C. S., & Comer, J. P. (1973). Racism and mental health services. In C. V. Willie, B. M. Kramer, and B. S. Brown (Eds.), *Racism in Mental Health.* Pittsburgh: University of Pittsburgh Press.

Thomas, A., & Sillen, S. (1972). *Racism and psychiatry.* New York: Brunner/Mazel.

Toldson, I. L., & Pasteur, A. B. (1976). Therapeutic dimensions of the Black aesthetic. *Journal of Non-White Concerns in Personnel and Guidance, 4*(3), 105–117.

Tyler, F. B., Sussewell, D. R., & Williams-McCoy, J. (1985). Ethnic validity in psychotherapy. *Psychotherapy, 22,* 311–320.

Tyler, L. E. (1965). *The psychology of human differences.* New York: Appleton-Century-Crofts.

U. S. Bureau of the Census, Department of Commerce. (1989). *Statistical Abstracts of the United States: 1989 (10th edition).* Washington, DC: U. S. Government Printing Office.

Vansertima, I. (1976). My Gullah brother and I: Exploration into a community's language and myth through its oral tradition. In D. S. Harrison and T. Trabasso (Eds.), *Black English: A seminar.* New York: Lawrence Erlbaum.

Vansertima, I. (1976). *They came before Columbus.* New York: Random House.

Vasina, J. (1971). Once upon a time: Oral traditions as history in Africa. *Daedalus, 100*(2), 442–468.

Walters, G. D. (1983). Racial variations on the MacAndrew Alcoholism Scale of the MMPI. *Journal of Consulting and Clinical Psychology, 51*(6), 935–936.

Walton, S. (1970). Census 70: Blueprint for repression. *The Black Scholar, 1*(3), 28–34.

Watson, J. B., and Rayner, R. (1920). Conditioned emotional reactions. *Journal of Experimental Psychology, 3,* 1–14.

Watts, T. D., & Wright, R. (1984). Some reflections on Black alcoholism treatment. *Journal of The National Medical Association, 76*(2), 101–102.

Webster's Third New International Dictionary. (1971). Chicago: William Benton.

Wechsler, D. (1944). *The measurement of adult intelligence.* Baltimore: Williams.

Wechsler, D. (1949). *Wechsler Intelligence Scale for Children; Manual.* New York: Psychological Corporation.

Wechsler, D. (1955). *Wechsler Adult Intelligence Scale Manual.* New York: Psychological Corporation.

Wechsler, D. (1974). *Wechsler Intelligence Scale for Children—Revised.* New York: Psychological Corporation.

Weiss, R. W. (1973). *Loneliness: The experience of emotional and social isolation.* Cambridge, MA: MIT Press.

Wesson, K. (1978). Toward a Black psychology. An annotated bibliography. In R. Jones (Ed.), *Sourcebook on the teaching of Black psychology, Volume 2.* Washington, DC: Association of Black Psychologists.

White, J. L. (1984). *The psychology of Blacks.* Englewood Cliffs, NJ: Prentice-Hall,

Williams, B. (1984, January). *Cultural differences and Black academic achievement: A scientific theoretical appraisal and practical implications.* Paper presented at the meeting of the New Jersey Chapter, Association of Black Psychologists, Princeton, NJ.

Williams, C. A. (1977). Black urban consumer cooperatives: Why they fail. (Doctoral dissertation, Rutgers University, 1977). *Dissertation Abstracts International, 38*(5), 3071A.

William, L. N. (1981). *Black psychology.* Washington, DC: University Press of America.

Williams, R. L. (1973). Abuses and misuses in testing Black children. In R. Jones (Ed.), *Black psychology.* New York: Harper & Row.

Williams, R. L. (1981). *The collective Black mind: An Afro-centric theory of Black personality.* St. Louis: Williams and Associates.

Winston, P. K. (1970). *The dialect of the Black American.* Berkeley Heights, NJ: Western Electric Company.

Wolberg, L. R. (1954). *The technique of psychotherapy.* New York: Grune & Stratton.

Wolfgang, M. E., & Cohen, B. (1970). *Crime and race: conceptions and misconceptions.* New York: Institute of Human Relations Press, American Jewish Committee.

Wortman, C. B. & Loftus, E. F. (1988). *Psychology.* New York: Alfred A. Knopf.

Wright, B. J., & Isenstein, V. R. (1978). *Psychological tests and minorities* (DHEW, Publication No. AOM78482). Washington, DC: U.S. Government Printing Office.

Wright, H. H., Scott, H. R., Pierre-Paul, R., & Gore, T. A. (1984). Psychiatric diagnosis and the Black patient. *Psychiatric Forum, 12*(2), 65–71.

Yetman, N., & Steele, C. (1971). *Majority and minority.* Boston: Allyn & Bacon.

Young, W. (1970, March 2). Make sure that Black counts in the 1970 census. *Trenton Times*, p. 10.

Index

About the Author

Lawrence N. Houston is a faculty member at Rugers University, where he serves as Professor of Africana Studies, Adjunct Professor of Psychology, and Joint Appointee in the Graduate School of Applied and Professional Psychology. Born in Philadelphia, Pennsylvania, he holds the Bachelor of Science and Master of Science degrees in psychology from Howard University and the Doctor of Education degree in counseling psychology from Temple University. Licensed as a practicing psychologist in Pennsylvania and New Jersey, he also is certified as a school psychologist in both states. In addition, he holds the Diploma in Clinical Psychology, awarded by the American Board of Professional Psychology (ABPP). In New Jersey, he has served as Professor of Psychology at Trenton State College, Senior Psychologist at the Annandale Correctional Institution and Superintendent at the Highfields Residential Treatment Center. He has provided consulting services in a wide range of settings, and his current research focus is on the prediction and enhancement of academic achievement among Black college students.